John Pepper's
ILLUSTRATED
ENCYCLOPEDIA
OF
ULSTER KNOWLEDGE

Illustrated by
Ralph Dobs

another Appletree haunbook

First published and printed by
The Appletree Press Ltd
7 James Street South
Belfast BT2 8DL
1983

10 9 8 7 6 5 4 3 2 1

British Library Cataloguing in Publication Data
Pepper, John
  John Pepper's illustrated encyclopedia of
  Ulster knowledge.
  1. English language—Dialects—Northern
  Ireland
  I. Title
  427'.9416   PE2586

ISBN 0-86281-118-X

For Bettie, in acknowledgment of the helpfulness of a wife able to accept without a grumble the persistent pounding of a type-writer—just one of the tribulations built into life with an author.

Foreword

As a rule an encyclopedia is not classified as a humorous work. This collection of facts about Northern Ireland is an exception. It seeks to show just how going shopping, buying a postage stamp, worrying about a budgie, itemising a soccer team's deficiencies, offering a cup of tea, can amusingly betray character and outlook.

Presented in these pages is a distillation of the behaviour, practices and routine described to me by a host of correspondents and those I have observed over a number of years. The tastes of the people, their lively use of language, their uniqueness and wit—all are here.

If there is a degree of emphasis on the vernacular this is because it is not really possible to provide a considered assessment of anyone without directly quoting what they have said and how they said it.

John Pepper

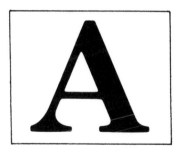

An awareness of the manner in which this letter can be ill-treated is essential for a proper appreciation of the Ulster vernacular and its eccentricities. While it is used normally in words like *pat, hat* and *mat*, it is constantly misemployed to produce *gat* for *got, hat* for *hot, lat* for *lot,* and *rat* for *rot,* as in 'that's a ratten oul day'. *Shap* is heard when *shop* is intended and *doctor* is transmuted into *dacter*.

Anyone named Scott will be addressed as *Mr Scatt*. It may turn Mr Scott blue in the face but there is nothing he can do about it. He is as helpless as Mr Potter who has to recognise that many people refer to him as *Mr Patter*. A dish of porridge will be *a plate aff parritch*.

A holidaymaker sun-bathing on the beach at Portrush with his daughter heard a jazz programme on a nearby transistor, suddenly recognised one of the tunes, and said, 'That's Nat King Cole'. Immediately the girl asked, 'Who is it then?'

A Belfastwoman told a friend, 'It was that hat my husband left aff his simmet'. A different note was struck when a newly-appointed hospital matron asked a patient how he was feeling. 'Ach, I'm not so hat,' he replied, indicating that he could have been better. She turned to a nurse and said, 'Get this man another blanket.'

ABYSS Approximates to the divide which distinguishes the working-class Ulsterman from those who consider themselves 'upper-class types'. The UCT can usually be identified by their shrewdness, a frequent tendency to be avaricious, the fact that they rarely wear a hat, dislike *Coronation Street*, are not regular church-goers, are enthusiastic about golf, squash, bridge and rugby, and sometimes *Match of the Day*. They would restore hanging, are mad when they read of the activities of people like Arthur Scargill, have no interest in pub darts, drink gin and tonic, 'Black Bush', or Bacardi and Coke, insist on their daughters having piano lessons, and usually have a stock of stories which they sometimes tend not to tell too well.

They are particularly fond of Ballymena stories and will simulate the accent to tell of the defence witness in a case in which a man was charged with injuring a neighbour by throwing a stone at him. Seeking to establish the size of the missile counsel asked, 'Was it as big as your fist?' 'It was bigger.' 'Was it as large as your head then?' 'It was bigger but it was nae as big as yours.'

As an encore there might be the story of the man conducting his own defence who was told, 'You may challenge any member of the jury now being called.' 'Right,' he replied, 'I'll fight that wee cross-eyed mon fornest ye.'

The average UCT tends to refer to himself as 'yours truly', and will frequently address you as 'Squire'. Likes starting statements with 'actually', has never been to a wake in his life, and is fond of sailing.

Will have days of quiet amusement thinking about it after being told of the Belfast boxer who said of an opponent, 'He'll give me no bother. He has an Achilles' heel. It's his jaw. It's made of glass.'

ADVICE When this is sought it is advisable to be aware of certain conventions. If you are approached by a native his inquiry will often sound rather more like a challenge, as in, 'You don't know where Durm Street is?'; 'You don't know the right time?'; 'You wouldn't have a match on you?'; 'You wouldn't have change of a poun on you?'

Similarly if you seek guidance to get to your destination you should be prepared for answers that are not quite straightforward. If you ask where a particular street might be you are apt to be told, 'Keep on the way you're going and you'll know it by the wriggly tin', in other words, by the corrugated iron fencing.

A motorist in Co. Londonderry who lost his way was advised, 'Ye'll hae to turn the car rount and go on down to the bottom of the hill there and take the road that lies till your left haun. Then if you don't lose the bap ye'll get there soon enough.'

Another motorist was left none the wiser when told, 'Keep on down the road and watch out on the right till you come to a big cheeser tree a couple of spits from Brannigan's pub where you'll see a big wide road. Don't go down it. The road you want is away past that on the left. Just ask anybody.'

AFTERNOON It is useful to know that this is a time of day rarely spoken of. Whereas elsewhere it is usually taken to mean the period between two and six o'clock p.m., this is generally referred to as evening in Ulster. In

England, 'long winter evenings' will be mentioned. In Ulster it is 'short winter evenings and long winter nights'.

ANSWERS There is much evidence of a tendency to avoid a direct 'yes' or 'no' when anyone is asked a question. People will feel awkward not so much because a straight question is put to them but rather by reason of their resentment at being forced to give a reply. A stranger who seeks to make sure he is on the right road for a bus station will never be given instant confirmation. Rather he will be asked in turn what is his destination and why, where he came from, did he enjoy himself, does he have any family. Finally, curiosity satisfied, the information he seeks will be provided.

When the question is inane the inclination to use irony in reply is rarely resisted:

'Haven't I seen your face before?' 'Probably, I've had it a long time.'

'Your head's bandaged. Did you get hurt?' 'I have a headache and the chemist asked me to try this as he was out of aspirins.'

'Are you limping?' 'No, this is a new dance step I picked up.'

'That's a nice tan. Are you back from your holidays?' 'You could be right. I thought this place looked familiar.'

'Somebody said your wife had left you. Has she?' 'No she's just gone to the Isle of Man for a fortnight with the windy cleaner. I'm on the pig's back.'

ANTRIM, COUNTY (pop. 352,549) A county in which the influence of the Scottish Presbyterian settlers is still strong. Pipe band music has a considerable following although this cannot be said of the kilt.

A mother commented to a neighbour, 'The wean went oot to school this mornin greetin buckets.' Clearly the child was not a dedicated scholar.

A caller at a North Antrim farm was told by the woman of the house, 'Come on on in an see the boss lyin on the sofa spillin his breath.' He was having a sleep.

On one of the rare occasions when Lough Neagh was frozen a villager said, 'If a hadda knew the Lough was friz ah'd have went to have saw it.'

When the inexorable happens the comment will be made, 'It betabe', and if someone says, 'twarthy', they mean two or three.

A gardener, bothered by the havoc caused by wood pigeons on his broad beans, asked in a pet shop for a 'board net to stop the boards from aitin my bains'.

A small boy who found a dead owl took it to his mother, who shouted, 'Take that oul ool oot o' here.'

A herd of cattle will usually be described as, 'A clatter o' bastes.'

A shopper, when told the price of an article was £1.10 said, 'I'm sure you'll throw off the 10p.'

11

'Missus,' he said. 'If I could throw off 10ps I'd be in the kitchen w' my heed ower the sink.'

County Antrim people know when it is St Andrew's Day and Burns' Night but they will not normally be adept at throwing the caber.

A party of German tourists travelling by bus stopped briefly in Ballyclare where they visited a local cafe. A resident, asked afterwards what he thought of them, said, 'A hevney muckle opinion about any yin thet disney speak the same as werselves.'

ARSE Slang, all-purpose term generally avoided by the middle-class, who will refer to the 'rear end', sometimes 'the posterior' or 'the bottom'.

A woman, grumbling at the difficulty of keeping her small son neatly clothed, said, 'I bought him a pair of trousers and he had the arse outa both knees before you could say Jack Robinson.'

A short distance will be covered by, 'It's not a kick in the arse down the road', and someone who walks aimlessly around will be summed up by 'All he does is arse about', or, 'He's never done arsin' about the lawn.'

A man who slipped and fell declared, 'I lit on my arse', while a decision to take no action will be conveyed by, 'I didn't bother my arse.'

A bore will be 'A pain in the arse', and, 'Arse about face' is another way of saying 'back to front.'

(see BEHINE)

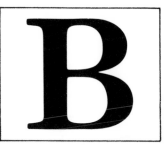

BACK   Normally this means the rear of the house, as in, 'They broke into my back', although a query at the grocer's, 'What's your back like?' betokens an anxiety to find out if the bacon can be recommended.

'He lives up my back', shows that the back of the speaker's house is in close proximity to his own.

'Back up' is an instruction to a horse to reverse. 'Back away there' directs the animal to continue to do so. 'To back a horse' is another matter and specifies that money has been placed on the animal in the hope of a considerable financial return.

A hairdresser asked a customer, 'Do you want your hair cut down the back?' He replied, 'Isn't there enough room where we are?'

A man who grumbled, 'The wife's never aff my back', merely echoed a common whinge.

BALLYMENA   Co. Antrim (pop. 55,000). Sometimes called 'Disneyland' because of the constant references to it heard there, as in, 'The child disney like her breakfast', 'My man disney like Tap Aff th' Paps. Says it sickens him', 'I asked the wife to come for a walk but she disney want to.'

The idiom embraces such verbal peculiarities as, 'We'll go down to the chinky for a snake', otherwise a light meal at the Chinese takeaway. Also to be heard is, 'He's a quack doctor', indicating that the speaker's general practitioner makes his decisions quickly, not that the man is unqualified.

'I spoke to the head yin', implies a discussion with the boss.

Ballymena is a paradise for anyone interested in *quent speech*, i.e. the quaint use of English. Much of it is of Scottish origin, thus giving rise to the town's reputation for prudence. There is, however, no justification for the suggestion that the statement, 'I shook hands with a friendly Arab. I still have my hand to prove it', could equally have been said of a Ballymena man.

The natives are kind-hearted and hard-headed, devout, concerned with what the neighbours think about them, but insist on value for money.

The man who complained about the soda farls bought in a home bakery, 'Them boys is stale. Them boys is yesterday's,' was merely standing up for his rights, demonstrating, 'You hae the wrang soo by the lug this time.'

In the rich farmlands surrounding the town people will speak of 'having a coo or two', indicating possession of a formidable herd of valuable cattle. 'A wee bit of land'

could embrace anything up to 200 acres. 'That's a fine yo' connotes a first class ewe 'worth a bit of money'. A stockbroker is a dealer in 'stocks and shears'. A woman shopper who asked for 'curn jam without curns in it' was seeking blackcurrant jelly.

BANAGHER Banagher Glen in the Roe Valley has an old parish churchyard in which an ancient Irish saint, St Muirdeagh, is supposedly buried. Sand from the grave is considered to have magical properties in warding off misfortune on the grounds that 'the sand of Banagher bates the divil.'

A reputed cure for a cow which has stopped giving milk is to wrap a leaf of the Bible containing a small quantity of Banagher sand round its horn. It was the answer to the milk blinker, someone able to cast a spell on a milking cow.

To declare, 'That bates Banagher and Banagher bates the devil', is to indicate astonishment at a happening or an argument.

To say of a comic 'That fella bates Banagher', points to his excellence as an entertainer.

BAX This has become the equivalent of an altar in the home. It holds all ages and all sexes in its grip, the worship starting at an early hour and lasting until after midnight.

The Belfastwoman who said, 'My oul lad clacks in front of the bax all night', was not describing someone out of the ordinary.

There are other meanings for the word, however. A woman will say, 'When our Jimmy goes aff till his work ye can see the wee bax strapped on the back of his bike for his samwitches.' In the same vein is, 'The oul lad has a wee plastic bax for his piece. A blue one.'

There is a different meaning in 'I gave the wee lad a bax on the ear.' The message here is that he has been misbehaving.

There is a common weakness for putting people 'in their bax'. It conveys a minor triumph as in 'I gave her a piece of my mind. That

put her in her bax all right.'

BEHINE Uttered with special emphasis on the last syllable, this is the equivalent of the French *derrière*, and the English *backside*.

A woman will say admiringly of her baby grand-daughter, 'She has her mother's behine.'

The expression figures in such statements as, 'He give me a dunt and I landed on my behine in the trinket', and, 'That lad wasn't behine the dure when the brains were given out.'

Other variants include, 'When that woman plants her behine in your house ye may say goodbye to Carnation Street,' and 'That's a quare wet day. A day like that and ye cud be gutters up to the behine.'

It was used during a shopping expedition by a Co. Tyrone man in search of a china dog for his mantelpiece. 'It fell and got broke,' he explained. 'Do you want a right-hand dog or a left-hand one?' he was asked. 'I don't rightly know,' he replied. 'All I can tell you its behine points straight down the main street in Portglenone.'

The comment was made of a man of unduly small stature: 'His behine should have a sweet enough smell, for it's brave and near the daisies.'

Said of a girl on becoming engaged to a man considered by the speaker to be of poor character: 'If that poor girl has burned her behine, it's her who'll have to sit

on the blisters.'
(see ARSE)

BELFAST (pop. 305,600). City of contradictions, statues and strong convictions. The rows of kitchen houses are gradually being replaced by more attractive homes whose tenants are apt to explain, 'the yard's upstairs', a tribute to the fact that there is no outside toilet.

Ulster poet Bill Nesbitt wrote these lines about it in 1968 and finds them still regularly quoted, constantly in demand. They were read on an Ulster radio programme and the BBC sent more than 800 copies to listeners who wrote asking for them:*

> I'll speak to you of Belfast, stranger, if you want to know,
> So listen, and I'll tell you why I love this city so…
>
> BELFAST… is an Ulsterman, with features dour and grim,
> It's a pint of creamy porter, a Sunday morning hymn,
> A steaming pasty supper, or vinegar with peas,
> A little grimy café where they'll serve you 'farmhouse' teas,
> A banner on July the Twelfth, a sticky toffee apple,
> An ancient little Gospel Hall, a Roman Catholic chapel,
> A *Telly* boy with dirty face, a slice of apple tart,
> A fry upon a Saturday, hot 'coal-breek' on a cart,
> A Corporation gas-man, complete with bowler hat,
> A wee shop on a corner with a friendly bit of chat,
> An oul' lad in a duncher, a woman in a shawl,
> A pinch of snuff, a tatie farl, a loyal Orange Hall,
> A tobacco smell in York Street, a bag of 'yella man',
> An Easter egg that's dyed in whin, a slice of Ormo pan,
> A youngster with some sprickly-begs inside a wee jam-jar,
> A meeting at the Custom House, an old Victorian bar,
> Mud-banks on the Lagan when the tide is running low,
> A man collecting 'refuse', bonfires in Sandy Row,
> A bag of salty dullis, a bowl of Irish stew,
> And goldfish down in Gresham Street, a preacher at a queue,
> A portrait of King Billy upon a gable wall,
> A flower-seller on a stool outside the City Hall,
> A half-moon round a doorstep, a 'polisman' on guard,
> A pedlar crying 'Delph for Regs!', a little whitewashed yard…
>
> And there's your answer, stranger, and now I'm sure you'll see
> Why Belfast is the only place in all the world for me.

It will never dawn on a Belfast-woman who tells her husband, 'I saw Mrs McCluggage coming through the window', that she might be taken literally. Nor are the words, 'That left fut of the wife's isn't near right yit', considered ambivalent.

Two nuns passed a Belfast woman and her small son in a Dublin street. The boy asked,

* Reproduced by permission of the author.

'What d'ye call them, ma?' 'For Gawd's sake,' she rebuked him, 'houl yer tongue or they'll know we're not one of them.'

A Belfastman whose house suffered severe flooding told a friend, 'It was terrible. I was just in time to save a soda farl from going down a third time.'

An East Belfast woman angrily told her small son as he was about to dash across a busy street, 'Come here this minute. D'ye want to get yerself kilt like they advertise on TV?'

Also typical was the comment of the woman whose husband was papering a room with wallpaper that had a complicated pattern of ducks and geese. When she arrived to inspect the finished job the floor was littered with left-over pieces. 'Man dear,' she exclaimed. 'Ye hev enough ducks and geese left to keep us in broth for a month.'

Usually pronounced *Bēlfast*, with the accent on the first syllable, but experts insist it should be *Belfāst*, with the accent on the second.

BIRTH Friends will say of a pregnant woman, 'She's thon way.' This is a condition which gave rise to the inquiry, 'Do I have to be seduced to be able to claim infertility benefit?'

Another pregnant patient queried anxiously, 'Will I have to have a sectarian birth?'

Of a mother with a child born out of wedlock it will be said, 'She's not married. She just had it.'

BIT This figures persistently in Ulster speech. Rather than announce the purchase of a new overcoat a Co. Antrim man will say, 'I bought myself a bit of an oul coat.'

A Co. Tyrone speaker will 'take a bit of a look at a new car,' and refer to a young woman as 'a bit of a girl'. 'A bit of a night' means one marked by much jollification.

Approval will be indicated by the statement, 'It's a bit of all right.'

Other usages include, 'He's a bit of an ijit', 'I'm going for a bit of a walk', and 'I gave her a bit of my mind.'

The statement, 'It's a bit down the road', can mean anything from one mile to five.

A person who says 'not a bit of it' is indicating violent disagreement with whatever opinion was put to him.

BLESSINGS While a blessing is the least expensive way of indicating appreciation this is no reflection on the sincerity and colour which generally goes with one. If blessings are going out of fashion it is because they can often be so fulsome and suspiciously flowery as to embarrass the recipient. 'May the devil never hear of your death till you're safe inside the gates of heaven', and, 'May every hair of your head turn into candles to light your way to paradise', would make most people squirm.

Today's blessings avoid the unctuous and run to the familiar, 'May your shadow never grow less', or 'May you be dead a year before the devil hears about it.' Satanic allusions, however, are going out of fashion.

Much depends on the reason for this style of expressing goodwill; whether, for example, it voices gratitude for a loan, a wage increase, or the provision of a drink when dying of thirst. 'May God put a strong thatch on that head of yours', and, 'May a doctor never earn a pound aff ye,' are acceptable but not really taken seriously. There are still followers in country districts of 'May the wind be always at your back', and 'May you rest in piece but not in pieces.' Dated blessings are, 'May you live that long that the skin of a gooseberry would make a skirt for you with seven flounces in it', and 'May you live till a goose-gab skin makes you a nightcap.'

A modern businessman would have some other device for wishing his obliging bank manager well than by saying, 'May misfortune follow you all your days and never catch up with you.' It would be more realistic to explain, 'May your giving hand never wither.'

BREADMAN The man who delivers the bread is as traditional a figure in domestic life as the milk-man. As in a home bakery, he may have on offer an infinite variety of delicacies, from a 'sore head' to 'a flies' cemetery', a 'sliced pan' to 'gravy rings'.

In some areas a request for a 'duck's neb' will mean that a Vienna roll is wanted. An order for a 'fresh lodger' indicates that a cylinder-shaped loaf marked off in half-inch slices is sought.

A well-stocked bread-van will carry soda and wheaten farls, crusties, fadge (otherwise potato farls), sliced pans, rolls, and pious buns.

A competitor in a bakery contest who failed to win a prize for his sodas was told that two of the three judges were from England. 'What wud ye expect,' he protested indignantly. 'What wud a coupla ijits of foreigners know about sodas?'

In many households this saying is still looked on as Gospel: 'Ate the crusts. They'll make you wise', which implies that they are conducive to frugality and thrift.

BUTCHER A trader who needs to have his wits about him to cope with sharp-tongued customers. His shop is a popular platform for pointed comment.

A boy returning a pound of steak said, 'My da says he could sole his boots with that.' The butcher sourly asked, 'Why didn't he then?' and was told, 'Sure he cudden get the nails through it.'

In a case where tripe was in little demand a customer was persuaded to give it a trial. Later, when asked how she liked it, she said, 'To tell you the truth my heart didn't lie to it so I gave it to the dog.' The outraged trader replied, 'Don't tell me he turned up his nose at it as well.'

A Newtownards butcher, when given an order for a sheep's head, was told, 'Leave the eyes in to see us over the weekend.'

In a village butcher's a customer remarked, 'Isn't it just beautiful here. Some day I would just love to be laid to rest in the nice wee churchyard down the road there.' Politely the butcher said, 'You'll be very welcome I'm sure, missus. We'll give you a funeral you'll never forget.'

If a customer says, 'My man's dead nuts for rose munn', a butcher will know instantly that her husband is a roast mutton buff.

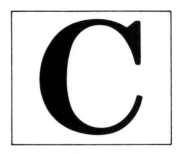

CAP Chiefly but not exclusively male headgear, sometimes known as a duncher. It has been hit by the vogue for bare heads.

Caps come in various styles. There are those which can be folded and kept in the pocket when the occasion demands, and others of more formal design suitable for a hallstand or hanging in a cloakroom.

A definition of a gentleman runs, 'He hangs his cap on the hallstand. He doesn't sit on it.'

One style inspired the comment 'That fella's cap lucks like a landin' pad for pigeons.'

There are men who wear their caps inside the house as well as out. A bareheaded Belfastman encountered on a pouring day was asked why he wasn't wearing one and said, 'Sure I came into town to buy myself a new one.' To the inquiry, 'But why aren't you wearing it then?' he answered, 'Sure I cudden sit around the house in a wet cap.'

A compliment is intended when it is said of a person, 'If you were in trouble he'd think nathin of puttin his cap roun for ye.'

A woman in an Armagh supermarket was heard to say, 'My husband went out without his cap and the wine was that fierce he came home with his head blown aff him.'

A woman who had a small boy by the hand asked in a hat shop, 'Can I have a cap to fit the wee fella? He has a square-shaped head like his da but if a round cap fits him I'll just take it.'

CHARACTERS These are in plentiful supply even if the comment is constantly heard, 'There aren't so many characters these days.' Every district has its own examples.

Down the years Belfast has produced 'Happy Jimmy', who toured the streets playing hymns on a hurdy-gurdy; 'Forty coats', so called because he went out with at least four or five ragged coats to keep him warm; 'Cowboy Joe', who cycled round the streets wearing a stetson, and riding as if his mount was a Wild West horse; and 'Choke the ducks', a religious oddity who roamed the city centre, with a Bible under his arm, and whose response to the jeers of small boys was to kneel on the pavement and pray for his tormentors.

CHEMIST Someone expected to provide a cure for almost every known ailment or complaint on demand. Besides his professional qualifications, if he is to stay in business, he must have a sound knowledge of the idiom and its peculiarities.

He will cope with ease with such requests as, 'The oul lad's corns is stoonin. Cud ye givvus some of them plasters to shut his gub?'

He will be unfazed by the customer whose age was asked for and who retorted, 'Dammit man, it's a rub I'm after, not a death certificate.'

Nor will he be troubled by the request, 'Wud ye send it down? It's my feet, y'know.'

It is all part of his day's work behind the counter to be faced with the complaint, 'The tablets you said would put me back on my feet musta been the wrong ones for they've done nathin' but make me run to the back.'

Probably apocryphal is the story of the chemist who handed a customer a bottle with the words, 'If this doesn't work, come back and I'll have another go at making out the doctor's handwriting.'

A Co. Antrim chemist was told, 'I want something to worm a dog.' He produced a hot-water bottle.

'Are ye mad?' he was asked. 'The wee thing has worms. I want something to worm the poor animal.'

A Belfast woman who went into a Boots store in London and asked for some headache powders was handed a packet of sanitary towels.

A Tyrone chemist was asked, 'Could you give me something for my arm. It's that sore I haven't been able to put on me for a week.'

CHERRYVALLEY Belfast suburb associated with ostentatious speech, due mainly to the way in which Belfast comedian James Young used it as a vehicle for poking fun at people who spoke with a marble in their mouth. He would refer to it as 'Cherryvelley', where the residents got their 'herr done' and would ask for 'sperr ribs' in a Chinese restaurant. They would say 'the weather's ferr', declare they 'wouldn't derr' go to see a dirty film, and speak of 'going upsterrs'. They would buy 'a new perr of shoes', say 'I don't kerr very much for an omelette', and describe an acquaintance as 'a rerr type.'

In fact, the residents of Cherryvalley have every reason to be resentful of the reputation given them, and to insist that it is 'quite unferr'.

CHILDREN The new generation is an unpredictable and amusing as those in any other part of

Britain. At school they display the usual tendency to take things literally, with unexpected results.

A teacher was explaining to her class the uses of the different senses. A little girl who had chattered incesantly was given the order, 'Hold your tongue.' The teacher then went on to ask, 'What do we have noses for?' From another pupil came the answer, 'To wipe, sir.' It was then seen that the first child was sitting solemnly holding her extended tongue between her fingers.

A boy not long at school was going over, at home, the words he had been taught. His father, however, kept correcting him until the child finally burst out, 'You're trying to make an Egypt out of me, aren't you?' Dad had no answer.

Another new pupil arrived home to announce, 'A lady had twins on the bus.' To the startled inquiry, 'And what happened?' he replied, 'She was taking them to school.' He had the same gift for the unexpected as the boy who broke the lead in his pencil and called out, 'Miss, the wick has gone down.'

A youngster who wasn't at all musical was told to leave the singing class and join another group. Next morning his angry mother arrived, demanding an explanation. The teacher pointed out, 'I'm sorry but your son just doesn't have an ear for music.' Protested the mother: 'If that's the case sure he has a lug like a saucer.'

Although marital status is not usually associated with geography a boy whose task was to write what he had learned about two American rivers obediently penned: 'They are Mrs Sippi and Miss Souri.'

A five-year-old boy arrived home from school in tears and explained that teacher had asked all those who wanted to go to heaven to raise their hands. 'You raised yours, didn't you?' his mother inquired. 'No,' sobbed the boy. 'Sure you told me to come straight home.'

At a kindergarten party a little Indian boy said he had been absent from school because his mother had been away to 'bring home a new babby' and he had returned specially for the party. When it was sought to find out if the new arrival was a boy or a girl he looked puzzled, did not answer, and trotted off, but was waiting at the door when the teacher was leaving. Tugging her to one side he said confidentially, 'I don't know if it's a boy or a girl. They say it's a thing called a sister.'

Religious instruction is a minefield for curious, bewildered young minds.

In a Co. Antrim school in an area with a wide following for horse jumping there had been a lesson on the story of the ten lepers. 'Why did the lepers stand afar off?' the question was put. The answer came unhesitatingly, 'To get a good run for their lep.'

When a class was asked, 'What did the angel Gabriel say to

Mary?' it brought the suggestion, 'Hello, Mary. You're going to have a ba.'

A boy who was faced with the need to read a passage from St John starting, 'In the beginning was the word...' started off perfectly, but when he came to the next sentence he read, 'There was a man sent,' then paused before resuming, 'By God, his name was John.' He was sternly warned to mind his stops and commas in future.

One child, tested by his mother to find out what he had learned, said, 'It was about God sending Moses to rescue the Israelites from the Egyptians.' It was suggested he should tell her the details. He replied, 'She told me that when the Israelites reached the Red Sea Moses built a bridge and the Israelites trooped across before they could be hemmed in by the enemy tanks. Then when they all got across the bombers blew up the bridge.' Astonished, the parent demanded, 'Did the teacher actually tell you that?' With a shrug the boy replied, 'Gosh no, mum. If I told it to you her way you'd never believe it.'

Confronted with the query, 'What did Isaac do in the Bible?' a pupil said, 'He worked on the roads.' The embarrassed teacher later discovered that the lad's father, also called Isaac, was a road worker.

During an elementary lesson on geography at a primary school the nun who was teaching gave some facts about the Irish climate. She turned a blind eye to the normal damp weather conditions and tried to convince the class that in Ireland the sun always shone, saying, 'In summer it is very hot here.' She was left speechless by a retort from the back of her class, 'Aye, sister, and the sky gets so hot that it nearly always sweats.'

It became a matter of routine with a perpetual latecomer to call him before the class, ask his excuse, and an automatic caution would be delivered. One morning he was unusually late and was asked: 'What's the excuse this time?' He replied, 'The Council's laying a pipe-line along our road and they've dug a hole at the end of our lane. During the night a horse fell into it and they couldn't get it out. I had to wait till they shot it before I could get across.' Sceptically the teacher inquired, 'And did they shoot it in the hole?' Replied the boy, 'No, sir. They shot it in the head.'

In one home gramps was fond of constantly reminding his grandson about the changes in school life since he was a pupil. 'We had to do all our exercises on the slates,' he pointed out. 'Weren't you afraid of falling?' came the query. 'What do you mean?' asked gramps. 'Sure you said you did all your exercises on the slates,' persisted the child.

CLERICS There is a strong and intimate relationship between clergy and people. In rural areas a clerical visit is an occasion.

A young curate visiting an ailing member of his congregation told her, 'I'm pleased to see you do not repine at the sufferings providence has put upon you.' She replied, 'My rheumatism is bad indeed but I still thank heaven I have a back to have it on.'

A worshipper decided to go to church after a long absence and dressed specially for the occasion. The feathers in her hat were being tossed by the draught from a nearby window. The minister paused on his way down the aisle to welcome her and inquired if the wind was bothering her. 'It's all right,' she answered. 'I'll overcome that when the organ starts.'

A former vicar and his wife decided to attend a social in his old parish. 'I'm delighted to see you,' said his successor. 'And is this your most charming wife.' Quietly came the answer, 'This is my only wife.'

A Sunday school teacher, determined that her class would do well in an examination by the minister, rehearsed them carefully. Each was to be asked a question from the Shorter Catechism, starting with, 'Who made you?' 'God.' 'Of what are you made?' 'The dust of the earth', and so on. On examination day, as the class waited, the first boy asked if he could 'leave the room', and was still absent when the questioning began. The second boy was asked the first question:

'Who made you?' when he replied, 'The dust of the earth' he was told 'No, son. God made you.' Said the boy, 'You're wrong, sir. The wee lad God made is out in the toilet.'

A visiting minister enjoined a member of the congregation full of complaints, 'Always remember the good book tells us to be content with our lot.' Replied the man, 'That's the trouble. I haven't got a lot.'

A Roman Catholic priest encountered a party from the village who had been to an Orange demonstration. All were in good spirits. 'Did you have a good day?' he asked them good-humouredly. 'We did indeed,' came the answer. 'We had the time of our lives kicking the Pope up and down the field.' The cleric smiled and said, 'Well, it just served him right. He shouldn't have been there.'

A veteran member of a golf club with a reputation for lurid language was introduced to a visitor seeking a round, named Dr Abernethy. The visitor proved much the better player, the veteran as a result becoming progressively worse. With the game on the verge of being lost, the veteran found himself in one of the club's most notorious bunkers. As he studied his lie he called to his opponent, 'Doctor, before I play this shot—tell me, are you a DD or an MD?'

Among a Co. Down dean's unforgettable visitations was one where he had knelt to lead a parishioner and his wife in prayer.

A moment later their young son rushed in from the street in a cowboy hat, jumped astride the dean's back, and cried out happily, 'Gee up there.'

A Co. Antrim minister, learning that one of his flock was ill, told the man's wife that he would call to see him. 'But he mightn't know you, for he is randerin,' she pointed out. The cleric said he would call anyway and next day made the journey through snow and mud to a lonely farm at the back of Slemish. 'You came after all,' said the wife. 'I'm still feared he mightn't recognise you for he's still randerin.' However she led him into the bedroom where she announced, 'Now, John, who is this with me?' The man looked up. 'That's the Reverend John James Gilmore, the best and finest wee meenister we've had for a lang time,' he said firmly. The wife gave the minister a look. 'I told you he was randerin, Mr Gilmore,' she said.

CONVERSATION Dialogue, whatever the circumstances, can reach considerable heights of complication.

A man telephoned a tourist office and asked the cost of a room at a Ballycastle hotel and was told, 'Sorry. Our brochure with the details is not out yet.'

'When do you expect it?'

'I don't really know.'

'The hotel isn't in the 'phone book. Do you think I should 'phone Directory Inquiries?'

'I don't know.'

'You don't mind me asking these questions.' 'Not at all. That is what we're here for. If you don't ask you'll never know.'

On rather similar lines was the conversation between a passenger and a man in the ticket office at a rail station.

'Can I get a train here?' the passenger asked.

'I don't know about that. You can get a ticket.'

'I want to go to Bangor. What way are the trains running?'

'On the lines. There's one in ten minutes. If they're still there.'

These were the exchanges between an unexpected guest and her hostess:

'Ye'll take a drap a tay; a've just a taypot wet?'

'Naw, thank ye. I'm onny after me tay at home.'

'Ach away. Another drapa tay niver killed nobody.'

'Well, just ta plase ye. A cup in ma haun here at the fire, but mind ye a'm onny after a fry an sausages so a'm.'

'Sure a drappa tay is far sweeter, warmer and thicker than a cuppa tay any day.'

'Mebbe you're right.'

The factory's quiet wee man had notched up another small triumph, his sixth. Mother and child were doing well.

'Six. That's not a family, it's a private army,' said one of his workmates.

'Before long he'll be sayin it's cheaper by the dozen.' said another.

A third remarked, 'He'll be having a quare head count every night after this.'

To him, however, it was just another day. 'Right enough,' he murmured. 'It's wonderful what ye can gather up as ye go along.'

A woman carrying a dance frock over her arm on her way from the cleaner's was stopped by a friend who said, 'That's a lovely looking dress.'

'Aye, it's my going away one.'

'Going away? Where to?'

'Nowhere.'

'That's silly.'

'No it isn't. I'm leaving it by for the time my chin's tied up.'

Two women were discussing the husband of one of them and one asked, 'What's thon I see on your man's lip?'

'Ach, he just took a notion.'

'I thought for a wee minnit his eyebrow had dropped.'

'You may well laugh. That bittava tash he's tryin to grow is an oul nuisance. I giv him a bit av my mind before we came out.'

'Yiu were just right. It's diclus.'

'I tole him there was more hair on a goosegab. Now the oul ijit's in a huff and won't come out with me.'

An assistant at the pharmacy counter in a Belfast store faced a girl of sixteen and asked, 'Can I help you?'

'Smears.'

'What do you mean?'

'Smears.'

'What is it you'd like me to give you?'

'Swacks.'

'Is it painful?'

'No. Sard.'

The message the girl wanted to convey was that she had wax in her ears.

A Co. Antrim woman was telling a neighbour of a pain in her arm and complained, 'Heaven knows what it is.'

'Does it bother you much?'

'I can't get the toothpaste outa the tube.'

'Why don't you ask your daughter about it?'

'That wouldn't do any good.'

'After all she's a hospital nurse.'

'I wud never ask her. You'd be getting your jaws tied up before she'd even notice you were dead.'

COURTS Those involved in legal proceedings inevitably reflect local attitudes. A policeman, describing a visit to the home of an offender, said he had asked, 'Have you anyone else living here with you?' and was told 'Yes, my father and mother and his oul lady and oul lad.'

A Co. Armagh woman charged with assault was said to have bitten off part of the victim's ear. She was told, 'You are fined £5 and you will be bound over to keep the peace for six months.' Immediately she protested, 'I don't mind the fine. It's keeping the piece that bothers me. I spit it out and a dog ran away with it.'

An error was made in the Christian name of a man accused of a motoring offence. He decided not to go to court but arranged for his brother to be there to see what happened. There was silence when the offender's name was called. It was called again, then a third time, when a shout came from the gallery. 'There's no such man.' The court clerk retorted 'But who are you?' Back came the reply, 'I'm his brother.'

CURES Old-time cures still have a dogged following. Many people will resort to them before deciding on a visit to the health centre—and even after a dose of aspirins and the help of valium. Folk remedies exist for nearly every complaint, with the possible exception of a heart attack or a fractured skull. Cobwebs, starch, onions, vinegar, pepper, fat bacon, the cork of a whiskey bottle and a host of other elements are the simple requirements.

If a friend of a sufferer from warts said, 'I'll give you 2p for them,' and the coin was handed over, the transaction was considered an infallible method of getting rid of them, on the grounds that they had been sold. Another cure was to rub them with soil which would then be thrown after a funeral. 'As the corpse withers so will the warts,' was the thinking.

Cobwebs wrapped round a cut finger were looked on as certain healers, while a cure for mumps was to give a ferret a saucer of milk, wait while it drank most of it, and then give what was left to the sufferer. It had to be swallowed on the spot. A handy guide to survival took the form of a verse:

To cure whooping cough I'll tell you what,
Crawl under a donkey that's wearing a hat.
For a stoonin' corn there isn't a doubt
A bit of fat bacon will soften it out.
Should a fish bone ever stick in your throat
Down a raw egg and away it will float.

A little girl suffering from head sores was required to have her hair cut very short and the scalp covered with a poultice of thick starch, the hotter the better. Not quite in this category was the boy who couldn't keep food down. A woman with the same maiden name as his father had to give the boy a slice of buttered bread and jam. 'His stomach will be as right as rain in a day or two,' was the belief.

Another child nursing a sore throat was soon back to normal after being persuaded to eat an onion saturated with pepper. While he did so it was essential that a towel soaked in cold water be wrapped round his neck.

Getting rid of ringworm called for simple treatment in many homes. This consisted of dropping a˝ penny into a jar of vinegar, leaving it until the vinegar turned green, and rubbing the affected spots with the liquid. Usually the patient was assured that they could have the penny to buy sweets.

A sufferer from cold sores around the mouth could dab the sores with a cork soaked in the dregs of a bottle of Irish whiskey.

Getting rid of chilblains was no trouble if there was a baby in the house. All that was needed to banish them was to dab them with a baby's napkin—freshly wetted by the baby.

The older generation, it is suspected, spent endless hours trying out answers for this or that cause of domestic crisis. A glass of hot milk lavishly laced with pepper eased a stomach cramp. A soft corn between the toes could be disposed of by cushioning it from its neighbour with a piece of fat bacon. The white of an egg smeared over a cut stopped bleeding. A cure for a severe cough was to scoop a hole in a turnip, fill it with brown sugar, and slowly sip the juice.

A 98-year-old Comber pensioner was well known for his brew made from beer with the juice of boiled nettles, and stirred with a red hot poker. It was his regular nightcap.

Those who suffered from stomach pains which refused to shift had only to resort to the simple expedient of placing their shoes on the fender at night, with the heels turned towards the grate.

This was rather less complicated a procedure than a reputed cure for styes. This involved a married friend of the victim's mother touching them nine times with the edge of her wedding ring, turning the ring each time. Reckoned to be equally effective where an ulcer was the complaint was to take a raw egg in which the pounded shell was stirred.

The extent to which faith plays its part in reliance on folk cures is illustrated by the claim of the elderly Londonderry man who swore that catarrh would have made his life a misery but for his daily routine for keeping it at bay. Each morning, as soon as he rose, he would take three sips of lukewarm water 'in the name of the Father, Son and Holy Ghost'. The same incantation was used in many other cases where the cure had to be drunk.

A strongly-held belief in Tyrone was attached to the marriage of two people with the same surname. They were considered to have acquired an ability to charm away all kinds of pains and aches. A Tyrone woman of ninety-six asserted that she never had a doctor in her life because every time she had a complaint she would rub the spot with whiskey, then have a small glass herself, on the premise that 'a little inside and out is the best cure of all.'

It is seen that although the remedy was often as drastic as the distress it was designed to relieve, this did not dismay the patient. Still to be found are believers in a cure for a skin rash which entailed licking a frog's stomach three times and then spitting into a fire which had been burning for three hours.

There does not appear to be any record of an antidote for 'a pain in the neck'.

CUSTOMS These come and go, die away and are suddenly revived, only to fade away again. Ulster is richly endowed with them.

Many relate to a specific day of the week. It is unlucky to empty the grate, pick flowers, have your hair cut or cut it yourself on a Sunday. For some reason this does not apply to shaving.

Still remembered in many households is the old saying, 'Never cut your nails on the Sabbath morn or you'll rue the day you ever were born.'

To clean your windows on a Monday brings the risk of ill luck for the rest of the week. It is looked on as unwise to start a new job, set out on a journey or begin a task on a Friday.

Many people, when told they can leave hospital on a Saturday, will ask to be allowed to stay till Sunday. Saturday is also considered a day of ill omen on which

to move house. The basis in each case is the belief that, 'a Saturday flit means a short sit.' To bring peacock feathers or hawthorn into the house is also to ask for trouble. Misfortune is in store if you persist in stirring your tea to the right. Good fortune is sure to follow if you turn around the coins in your pocket when you see a new moon.

To have a brush thrown after you when you set out to be interviewed for a new job is considered a good omen. One woman said, 'When I left the house for an interview my husband threw a brush after me for luck and nearly broke my ankle. But I got the job.'

Another pre-interview custom is to put your left foot out first when you set off.

It is asking for trouble for two people to look into a mirror at the same time, or to take a photograph of a relative's grave.

A useful precaution during lightning is to place all the knives, spoons and forks on the kitchen floor.

The smell of roses is a certain cure for a headache and if a cat sneezes near a bride-to-be it means she will have a happy marriage.

Putting a new pair of shoes on the table can bring disaster, as can opening an umbrella indoors. To allow a red-haired person to first-foot you on New Year's morning also invites calamity.

When visiting a friend who has moved house a present of salt

29

should be brought and a few grains sprinkled in every room. This ensures 'a happy flit'.

Immediately someone dies the windows of the room in which they passed away should be opened to enable the spirit to depart.

If you own a hen which isn't laying, a certain remedy is to place some red flannel in the nest.

Still faithfully observed by many of today's bridge players is the custom of rising and walking round your chair as a remedy for bad hands. This was done in many rural areas by those who played less sophisticated domestic games like whist or ludo.

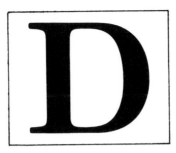

DEATH Reflecting the resigned approach to departure from this life, often encountered, is the comment of the aged Co. Antrim woman when told of the passing of yet another old friend: 'It looks as if the Almighty's forgot all about me.'

A tenant who had just moved into a small kitchen house was asked what she thought of it and replied, 'It'll do me my day. The only thing that's wrong with it is that you can't turn on the stairs. A coffin would never go up nor a corpse come down them.'

A bereaved husband, asked at the graveside how many were in the family plot, answered, 'She's the third, and if God spares me I'll be the fourth.'

On a stormy night a bus passenger commented to her companion, 'I'm thinking my ma's as well dead than running about on a night like this.'

A mourner at an Omagh funeral said of the deceased, 'She told me she was forty-nine but that must have been the number on her door.'

A Co. Down man decided to erect a monument to the memory of an uncle who had left him a generous legacy. He asked a monumental sculptor, 'How much would it take to put up a stane, say a word or two about him, and rail him in?'

Overheard at a Ballyclare funeral, 'Poor Minnie. There's one thing—the family didn't affront her. Look at them handles on the coffin. They're as long as your arm.'

The sexton in a poor parish in Co. Tyrone was consulted about the erection of a memorial on the church wall. 'It will be very welcome,' he replied. 'It will take the bare look off things. Please God we'll have room for more like it.'

When a widower returned dejectedly from his wife's funeral, his married sons and daughters tried to console him by saying he could stay with each of them in turn, and that he wouldn't be lonely. 'That's not what's worrying me,' he pointed out. 'I was just thinkin' about the oul ijit that I am, forgettin' to take aff herself's weddin' ring before she was buried when I cudda used it again.'

A minister returning from a funeral noticed a parishioner working in his garden, and said, 'I'm surprised you weren't at John's funeral.' 'Are ye?' came the reply. 'I didnae go to his funeral for he won't be going tae mine.'

A youth, sent to the undertaker's for a shroud, was questioned on the size required. 'Ah don't know the size. It isn't for masel,' he replied.

A Co. Tyrone man was told, 'That's a terrible bad cough you've picked up.' He answered, 'Ach, a don't know about that. There's people in the graveyard would be glad of it.'

A 'meals on wheels' volunteer called on a woman whose husband was awaiting burial. 'Where will I put the dinner?' she inquired. The widow pointed to the open coffin and said, 'Just put it in there, so long as you don't cover his face.'

As a funeral passed on a wet day the comment was heard, 'That's poor oul' Mary Dodds they're buryin'. Isn't the sowl gettin' a terrible day for it?'

(see WAKE)

DESPERATION Condition frequently experienced but indicated in different terms. 'I'm desperate for a drink', and 'He's desperate for a woman', imply the same degree of anxiety although they are not in the same class as 'The situation is desperate'.

A neighbour can be 'a desperate nuisance', while 'a desperate man' is usually someone who can easily get his companions into trouble during a night out, a person whose actions are unpredictable.

'A desperate speaker' describes an indifferent orator, an insufferable bore.

'Desperate weather' can embrace gales in June and snow in July, and 'a desperate job' connotes a lawn constantly in need of cutting by a reluctant gardener.

'I'm desperate' usually indicates an urgent desire to go to the toilet.

DOHERTY A name long associated in Tyrone, Armagh and Derry with a host of old-time sayings, many still to be heard. In Armagh, when the potatoes were cooking on the fire, the woman of the house would chant:

> The tatties are boilin and that's a great joke,
> For the herrins are comin in Doherty's boat.

The name figures in another common saying:

> Your grannie was a Doherty,
> True to the blood,
> And wore a tin nightcap,
> The time of the flood.

This was probably a nonsense verse used as a nursery rhyme to pacify children at bedtime.

DONKEYS Constantly used as an abbreviation for *donkey's*

32

years, otherwise a long period of time.

A motorist, upset at the non-delivery of a new car, will complain to the dealer, 'I'm fed up. I've been asking you for donkeys.'

A woman in a supermarket will protest, 'I've been waiting in this queue for donkeys.'

A Housing Executive applicant will insist, 'I've been coming here for donkeys.'

A Belfastman, angry that someone he had been trying to telephone always seemed to be out, insisted, 'I've been calling for donkeys.'

A secretary, who has spent hours searching for a letter to the boss which she has mislaid, will declare, 'I'm looking for donkeys.'

DON'TS Awareness of a number of these is invaluable for the stranger. Don't, for example, inquire 'Where?' if told, 'I haven't been.' Don't be tempted to ask ironically, 'Do you plan to put them on the mantelpiece?' if told, 'I bought a pair of shoes but they aren't for wearing.' This indicates they are for special occasions. They are in a different category to the pair bought by a woman, 'Just for walking behind the child's pram.'

It is asking for trouble to inquire, 'What's his position on the team?' when informed of a footballer, 'He uses the wrong fut.' This has the same meaning as, 'He digs with the wrong fut', which should not be taken to refer to a left-footed gardener.

If it is said of someone, 'He walks', it is unwise to inquire 'What's so strange about that? I walk to the office every day myself.' In all these cases the reference is to someone of a different religious persuasion to the speaker.

When buying a loaf at 10p and the shopkeeper offers you two for 19p, causing you to comment, 'That isn't much of a reduction', don't assume he is speaking literally if he says, 'Do you want jam on it?' The message is that you are expecting too much.

DOUBLE - BARRELLED NAMES John Willie and Samuel James are common varieties of the rural Ulster custom of giving children double-barrelled Christian names intended for regular use. Rugby international Willie John McBride is better known on the sports pages as Willie John than by his surname.

The same is the case with other bearers of this style of nomenclature, such as Samuel Joseph and William James. Their surnames are rarely used.

A wife asked by a caller seeking her husband 'Is Mr —— at home?' will often answer, 'Samuel James is down in the meadow', or, 'Samuel James is away upstairs to put his head down for a wee minute.'

Ulster kitchen comedies are full of examples of the custom. A double-barrelled name usually labels a member of the cast as a well-off farmer.

In those areas where *Hugh* is pronounced *Cue* (as distinct from Belfast, where the general form is *Shue*) it does not imply that Cue John is an expert snooker player. Women are not immune from the tradition, Mary Jane being the best known form.

The christening custom is common in North America, taken there by Ulster settlers. However, in many cases only the initial of the second name is used, producing such examples as William J., Donald T., and even Harry O.

DOWN, COUNTY (population 340,009). Embraces the Ards peninsula, noted for its pawkiness.

A man paying a call on a friend was told by the man's wife, 'He's in bed with a bile. He's giving me a pain in the behine moanin' about it.' In fact he was suffering from a boil.

A guest invited to have a cup of tea is apt to reply, 'A dinny like it in a cup—it is ower wee. A dinny like it in a tin—it's ower warm. A dinny like it in a bowl—it's ower thick in the lip. A wud rather hev it in a mug.'

A visitor in Newtownards arrived while the woman of the house was baking. Her small son was playing about in the room, causing the caller to say, 'Hi boy, yer breeks is a flure behine.' The lad's trousers, in other words, were marked with flour.

A motorist on tour asked a villager for directions to a destination beyond Saintfield. He was told, 'Feth, you're a brave wee wheen of miles from where you're headin', but you push on and you'll come till a loanin' on your left haun. Take the next by-road past that and it'll bring you as far as Sanfeel, and you'll be nearer where you went to go than you are here. Does that please ye?'

A traditional South Down rhyme runs:

The sun has set or sunk
The moon has rose or risen
He slowly put his haun in her's
And she put her's in hisen.

Illustrating Co. Down's way of putting things is the small boy who dashed into a Portavogie shop exclaiming, 'The Doreen Girl's just abin the harbour. She hes her heid doon like a soo an must be haying a hundred cran.' His message was that a local fishing boat was on its way in, loaded with herring.

If it is said of someone: 'He has piles', it should not be assumed he is suffering from haemorrhoids. On the contrary he is well off, a valued friend of his bank manager.

DRINK Covers every form of liquid refreshment, whether lemonade or liquor, porter or absinthe, stout or ginger ale, claret or Coke.

'There's a drink in it for you', promises anything from a pint of Guinness to a large Scotch as a reward for doing a job or a favour.

'Do you take a drink?' seeks to find whether or not there is a danger of you being an alcoholic and thus 'drinking the bit out'.

'Had he drink on him?' aims to establish if someone was (a) palatic (b) bluthered (c) flying (d) legless (e) putrid (f) as full as the Boyne (g) nicely (h) smashed (i) poleaxed (j) on the sauce (k) plastered (l) away w' the band (m) stovin (n) scuppered.

The inquiry, 'Watter ye hevvin?' is a serious invitation to accept hospitality, as is, 'You stannin?'

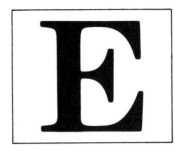

EDUCATED   To qualify for the compliment of being described as 'educated' calls for a wide range of attributes. You need to be 'well spoken', never talk about your bowels, go to the lavatory and not 'the classit' when the occasion demands, take one spoonful of sugar in your tea, not three or four, refer to 'rugger' not 'rugby', be able to 'fill in forms' without difficulty, and have a taste for smoked salmon when eating out.

A conversation between someone educated and someone who is not took place in a home bakery when a customer ordered, 'Six baps and six budgie rolls, and put them in separate begs.' He was asked, 'Is it the baps or the rolls in separate bags?' The reply was, 'Both.'

In the course of a discussion a visitor to the family murmured 'As Shakespeare said, "Man's inhumanity to man makes countless thousands mourn."' It brought the comment, 'Isn't it nice to have a wee bit of education.'

Of a youth whose conduct was considered exceptionally good it was said, 'He's not a bad boy at all. He's an obliging sort, and educated, too.' An immediate retort was, 'An ordinary young rascal you can keep your eye on, but the divil outa hell couldn't watch an educated one.'

Another definition of 'educated' surfaced when the statement was made, 'Tomorrow wid be the day about six weeks ago when it happened,' inspiring the comment, 'When she said that I knew she had a great head for dates. She mustav been a grate scholar.'

EXCUSES   There are illustrations galore of ingenuity in providing an alibi, explaining away a chronic inability to be punctual, or excusing forgetfulness. The gift is common to young and old.

A schoolboy pleaded, 'It isn't my fault I'm late, miss. My big sister bate me to the bathroom.'

Another claimed, 'My morr cudden get the car started. She called it an oul' bitch.'

Still around are the descendants of the boy who insisted he saw a notice saying, 'Mind the steam-

36

roller,' and argued, 'I minded it till the driver came.' Today's variants of this involve heeding injunctions to 'Mind the dog' and 'Mind the tar'.

Most common alibi is 'I slep in.' Tyrone people are as prone to this as Armagh, Antrim and Down folk.

Explanations for unpaid bills are wide-ranging. A woman whose husband was receiving sickness benefit wrote, 'I can't pay you anythink this week. My husband's sick hasn't come but the minnit it comes through the letter-box I'll let you have it.'

Said of a school absentee, 'I had to keep the wee lad aff for he was bunged up with the cowl. The snatters were trippin' him. I hope he doesn't smit the rest of them for there'll be the quare pantomime.'

A despairing appeal said,

'Please excuse Joe from staying for school lunch. He's rarin' a thrush and I can't stand cuttin up the worms.'

EXILES The exile doesn't exist who fails to prick up his ears at the sound of a familiar accent far from home.

A Belfastman who had settled in Bristol and set up as a taxi driver established an instant rapport with one exile by asking her, 'Whaur till?'

An Ulster couple shopping in London were discussing whether or not to buy some knitwear and came to the conclusion, 'We could get just as good at home and a bit cheaper.' A tall young man leaned towards them said 'Carract,' and moved on. 'That's made our day,' they decided happily.

FANLIGHT Semi-circular window over the front door of older style terrace houses. Often used to give personality to the abode and for the display of such evidence of this as a stuffed bird or artificial plants. An ostentatious householder will be contemptously referred to with, 'Her and her stuffed duck in the fanlight! Make ye sick.'

In some cases stuffed rabbits have been known but there were also stuffed parrots. Fanlight taxidermy, sadly, is dying out.

FEET A subject of constant preoccupation. Footlore is almost as extensive as folklore. The woman who complained, 'I'm walked aff my feet luckin' for wide fittins to let my bunions out', is not uncommon. One announced, 'I'm quaren careful with my feet since I was sick and the doctor told me he nivver knew till he got me into bed that I had pneumonia in them.'

Comment in a shoe shop: 'I've found out why it was John Bunyan who wrote the Pilgrim's Progress. Bunions would make anybody feel they were like pilgrims.'

Heard in a bus: 'My man said his new shoes were kriplin him and his big toe was as black as the ace of spades, so I towl him to lave them aff till he gat them broke in.'

A woman in a shopping queue who admitted she had 'bad feet' was given the advice: 'Go to the charapadist. Wire yer shoes is pinchin yer feet or yir feet is pinchin yer shoes go to the charapadist. I was there last week. Ingroan toe nail, hard skin, saft corn. He tuk them all away. My feet was like new.'

A woman commented witheringly, 'My oul fella will nivver hev athlete's fut for he nivver run a yard in his life.'

A shoe shop assistant was told, 'I gat a pair of them patient shoes and they're light in the haun all right but when you have them on they're like clogs. The price isn't aff the sole yet.'

Another customer declared, 'I have a neighbour and you can see the pain of her bunions on her

FEED THE PIGS IN THEM

face. See me? Them teetering heels is right for the young ones but I'll just stick till my wearin shoes.'

A man who said he saw a Linfield forward score with three headers insisted he was that good 'he had no need of his feet'.

A shopper in Londonderry vowed that, 'Them plastic shoes fairly draw your feet so they do.'

A woman badly cut by treading a broken bottle was carried to the doctor. As she was taken into the surgery she exclaimed, 'Oh doctor. You should see the bad hand I've made of my foot.'

After an exhaustive session with a customer who tried on nearly every shoe in the shop, the assistant was heard to say, 'I can't get that woman's feet outa my head.'

The woman who said, 'I wore them shoes for a week before I put them on', was indicating that she did not go out in them for that period.

Another request was for a pair of heavy boots, 'brave and strong for I have to milk the cows in them at six and feed the pigs in them at eight.'

There was once a demand for, 'A chape pair of shoes just for him to kick about the house.'

A woman told a friend: 'Just put your feet in a bus and you'll be welcome any time.'

Anyone who 'digs with the wrong foot' has religious beliefs not shared by the speaker.

A shoe shop assistant, when advised that the shoe a customer had tried on would satisfy him, said: 'Will you go to the front and see it your other foot's on the rack?'

A man coming out of a shoe shop said, 'I was trying on a pair and the girl said, 'They'd be a better fit if you took your socks off.'

FOCALS Strictly speaking these are spectacles with the lens made in two sections, but they also describe the songs provided by pop group vocalists, as in, 'Milly does some great focals', and, 'You should hear Kathy doing "When you and I were young, Maggie". She can fairly sing. The group would be a dead loss without her focals.'

FRY Generic name for a meal of fried eggs, sausages, bacon, soda and potato farls. The hotel, restaurant or boarding house where guests are given 'a fry for breakfast' is considered superior.

'He's dyin about a fry' is a man who is reckoned to know his onions.

'A fry puts you on your feet' connotes a meal guaranteed to 'warm the cockles of your heart'.

The woman of whom it is said, 'She knows how to do you a fry', can have no higher tribute paid to her.

A fry is outstanding for its flexibility. It can be served with a pot of tea for lunch, dinner or supper.

A man working in his garden who hears the call, 'Would you come in for your tea, it's a fry', is given a message which needs no translation.

Fried bread is also known as 'dip'. A Belfastwoman told a neighbour, 'When we were in Malta last year I asked the waitress could we have dip and she gave me a look. Only another woman told her what we wanted we could have been there yet.'

GLORY HOLE Space under the stairs in terrace-type houses. Used for the storage of household articles not necessarily discarded. A place for the child's bicycle, brushes, mops, shoes, slippers, sticks for the fire, dusters. Also used for hanging wet raincoats and setting the mousetrap. Known in some homes as the 'coal hole'. It is always unlit.

Obstreperous children would be threatened: 'If you don't be good you're for the glory hole.' It is the 'sin bin' in the households of today.

GOOD JOB When a North Antrim man says, 'It's a good job you did', he is not praising the job so much as seeking to draw attention to the serious consequences which would have followed if the action had not been taken. A young farmer who had just got engaged was met by a friend who said, 'A hear yer ganty merry Martie Magee?' 'I hope to—in the summer,' was the reply. 'Ah'll houl ye, me boy, she'll houl tae ye,' came the approving comment. It indicated that the girl would be able for her man at every turn. Years afterwards he was able to say, 'It was a good job I married Martie. We have had a grand time together and my friend was dead right.'

GREETINGS These take many forms and can often confuse the visitor. 'Har-ye?' voices friendly concern about the state of your health, as does 'You awri?' and 'Hunky dory?' 'Bite ye?' does not mean that the speaker is asking if the dog you have at your heels is liable to turn vicious. It is again showing an interest in how you are, a version of 'How about ye?'

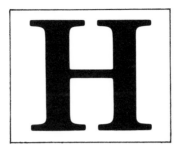

HALF Often crops up in statements intended to be ironic. 'He wasn't half bad' means he could have been a lot worse.

'He didn't half run', conveys that he went at a right lick.

'She didn't half give it to him', denotes severe censure.

'A man and a half', 'a dog and a half', 'a horse and a half', and 'a party and a half' are all examples of the exceptional.

On the other hand, to be 'half cut' is indicative of less than normal sobriety, and 'half dead' signifies extreme inactivity.

HARDWARE Owners of shops specialising in hardware take in their stride requests that call for real resource. Many of them are far from straightforward:

'I want a dog lead for my mother.'

'Could I see your earrings? I just got my ears permed.'

'Would you have a ball for this bloody wee bitch of ours?'

HEALTH A perpetual topic among both sexes.

Asked, 'Does your stummick bother ye as much?' A sufferer replied, 'Not after I got till sixty. The stummick just left me then.

At a health centre a woman told her friend, 'I'm still on the rhubarb and bran for I don't want to see thon dacter again if I can help it.'

Another overheard comment was, 'My man's not at all well. He's on a stick.'

One odd remark was, 'She says she's sufferin' from hallucinations but I think she's onny imaginin' it.'

A Co. Down farmer, describing an operation, summed it up in the words, 'They just took tools and wrought on me.'

A patient in a doctor's waiting room said, 'He's a great wee man. He gave my husband a cure for his piles and he hasn't looked behind him since.'

HOME BAKERY An institution in every shopping area, since bread has a role at practically all meals.

A woman returning an unsatisfactory purchase complained

43

AN ULSTERMAN WILL LAUGH HEARTILY AT HIMSELF

angrily, 'Call that a barm brack! Ye cud ride a bicycle through the curns.'

Some home bakeries will excel in wheaten bread, others in their soda farls.

A testimonial to one establishment ran, 'Not many cud houl a candle to it for the cake they soul me. Whatever they put in it—it ferly riz.'

A hostess will not hesitate to acknowledge that the cake a guest admires was not her own work. She will say quite frankly, 'Spaught', emphasising that there is nothing shameful about having bought it in a bakery.

HOUL One of the key words vital to an understanding of the complexities of the Ulster vernacular. If the reader can 'houl his hurry' he will learn that there is 'houl in', meaning restrain yourself, and 'houl out', meaning don't give in, 'houl back', implying wait, and 'houl forth', meaning talk. 'A houl you he's lying' expresses strong suspicion. There are motorists who 'houl till the crown of the road', and won't 'houl be the rules' to let a faster car pass. 'Houlin' a bus' means keeping it waiting until you're ready to go. 'Houl yer breath' is a request to stop and listen, and 'houl yer temper' is a plea not to get excited. 'Houl yer peace' and 'Houl yer tongue' are calls to take it easy, as is 'Houl on there', although this can be addressed by a horseman to his mount. An appeal not to 'houl it over me' expresses the wish that something you have done should not be cast up in a derogatory way. 'Houl yer fire' suggests that you should withhold criticism until you have heard an explanation. Anyone who agrees that all this will 'houl water' deserves praise for endurance.

HUMOUR The natives usually have a sharp sense of humour and, as a rule, can tell a story uncommonly well because of this. The Dubliner has wit, but his sense of humour has some deficiencies. He will not laugh at himself but will laugh at others. An Ulsterman will laugh heartily at himself. He will not see anything questionable if told of the customer in a Co. Down cafe who ordered, 'Two slices of toast, burnt as black as your boot, three slices of fat bacon half fried, and a cup of black coffee,'and then explained, 'A hev worms and anything is good enough for them.'

Statements will often be made to test the sharpness of the listener. This applies to a woman's comment in a fruiterer: 'See them bananas of his? If he doesn't get rid of them soon they'll be going'; and another which ran: 'Them tomatoes aren't fit for human constipation.'

To say of someone, 'They're a turn', is highly complimentary. They are the salt of the earth because they are 'good crack', are always good for a laugh, and can 'have you in fits.'

IDIOCY There are degrees of this state of mental inadequacy.

A 'buck ijit' can be defined as a literary critic who finds favour in the 'buck lep' school of Irish writing. He can also be a man who puts a lot of money on a horse which comes in last, votes for a candidate who has the lowest poll, or encourages his wife to go to a karate class.

'Buck ijits' can also be seen in television discussion panels, and on the soccer field. They can sometimes be heard reciting 'The tip of me oul cigar' at house parties. Many of them take up political careers.

INSULTS Colloquial speech is rich in insults. They embrace every known character deficiency, and cover all kinds of oddity.

A gossip is summed up in, 'She has a mouth like a pillar box—always open.'

A grumbling mother said of her son's choice of bride, 'My Johnny married a tin opener.'

A reply to the comment, 'She gave me a nasty look', can be, 'She had one before I met her.'

Other examples: 'He was that long getting his hand into his pocket I thought he was paralysed'; 'He's a slippy tit—even comes into the house like a drop of soot'; 'Mean? Him? You might as well look for the grace of God on a mushroom or wool in a goat house as expect him to pay his way'; 'He wouldn't open his mouth for fear he would waste his breath'; 'That woman has a voice that would crack a tay pot'; 'He's that near he stews his false teeth for gravy,'; 'She's that mangey she wouldn't give you two drops from her nose'; 'He wouldn't spit in your mouth if your teeth were on fire.'

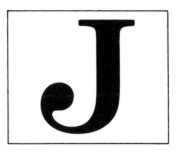

JAR A welcome drink; also a hot water bottle.

'You're always sure of a jar in Jimmy's', indicates that he is a man with 'a givvin' haun', a generous host.

An Ulsterwoman on holiday in Derby asked her English sister-in-law for a jar for her small son at bed-time. 'You start them young in Ulster, don't you?' she commented, making for the strong drink cupboard.

No alcoholic undertones are involved, however, in the suggestion, 'Leave the door on the jar.'

JOKER 'A joker and a half', or 'A bit of a joker', is someone who is perpetually striving to raise a laugh. They never tire of telling the story of the two Belfastmen sweltering in 91° on a Spanish beach on the 12th of July. One says 'I've just remembered the date. Man aren't they gettin' a great day for the Twelfth at home.' A joker will speak of an acquaintance as 'The kind of fella that would want to be put into the non-smoking part of a lifeboat', will say of the food in Majorca, 'It was all right but I got sick of the muckaroni', and is apt to make frequent allusions to: 'Big Sammy. Every time he gets back after a walk to the corner the hum of his feet is desperate.'

JUICE Before decimilisation this was the slang term for twopence, as in 'Lennus a juice'. If a car is 'heavy on the juice' its fuel consumption leaves something to be desired. 'Pickey juice' was once a slang description applied to Hebrews. Thankfully it is no longer heard.

LIGHT This has several different meanings.

A small boy with a cigarette asked a passer-by for a light and was sternly told, 'Run away home ye wee brat or I'll light ye on your behine.'

Someone who has suffered a shock will say, 'It took the light from my eyes.'

'I'm going to light out', indicates an imminent departure.

To be told at a soccer match, 'You're stannin in my light', specifically requests that you should move somewhere else or there'll be trouble.

Anyone on whom fortune

"HE CAN THROW YE AFF AFORE YER ON HIM!"

continually smiles 'always lights on his feet.'

LONDONDERRY (pop. 88,800). Second city in Northern Ireland. Sometimes known as the Maiden City. Residents who feel that gazetteers should have the city's entry cut by six letters and London scrapped, making it Derry, nevertheless usually acknowledge that there are problems in altering the title of the Londonderry Air. The girls somehow have never come to be known as Derry maids.

Sometimes known as the home of the 'surely folk', as natives seeking to indicate their agreement with a statement will say 'Aye surely'. They will do so if invited to have a drink, a cigarette, a cup of tea, or to go for a walk along the banks of the Foyle on a spring evening.

It is a city of hard-working, industrious people, the speech marked with a distinct lilt so that if a stranger asks the way the reply is said to sound so melodious that if you don't know the music you're lost.

It boasts a considerable number of *Daritys*, otherwise Dohertys.

Speaking of a pet pony a native said, 'He can throw ye aff afore yer on him. He just gives the head a jark, pulls the rains outa yer haun, and tosses ye over his head like a spinning jinny.'

Overheard at a city health centre: 'The wife can hardly spake way her beck. Now she's away to hospital way her nose.'

Of a couple going steady it will be commented: 'I saw them lunk arm in arm.' And to signal readiness for his breakfast a man will call to his wife from bed, 'Hate me trousis. A'm gettin up.'

MASTERMIND This BBC memory contest has produced many formidable Northern Ireland challengers. Its popularity has given rise to the legendary tale of a Belfast contender who set up a record in passes. It went like this:

'What is the name of a Belfast thoroughfare which starts with Donegal?'

'Pass.'

'What is needed to gain a seat in the Parliamentary Press Gallery?'

'Pass.'

'What kind of a book are you given when you open a deposit account at your bank?'

'Pass.'

'You are playing bridge and your partner bids one spade. You have no face-cards in your hand. What do you reply?'

'Pass.'

'How is a card described which allows you to travel free by train?'

'Pass.'

'You are driving along a motorway and a lorry in front of you slows down to five mph. What do you do?'

'Pass.'

'What does an Army sentry say to you if he has established your credentials?'

'Pass.'

'What word beginning with "by" describes a thoroughfare which circles round a town or village?'

'Pass.'

'What do you do with your water when you go to the toilet?'

'Pass.'

'A judge is delivering sentence. What will he do with it?'

'Pass.'

'What should a rugby player do with the ball if he wants to give it to a back?'

'Pass.'

'You are on a journey; what stage is reached which is covered by the term "pretty"?'

'Pass.'

'What is done in America if you want to get rid of a buck?'

'Pass.'

'You are a cleric seeking to indicate that an event has happened.

Where do you say it has come to?'
'Pass.'

MEDICINE   In many rural districts medicine means a laxative, probably because for years this was almost the only cure given. The advent of the National Health Service has changed things, but to many of the older generation the original meaning persists.

A Ballymena doctor will understand at once when a patient asks for 'medicine for my bools'.

'He's away to the doctor for a bottle,' similarly implies the need for medicine, whether a tonic or otherwise.

This usage is not to be confused with the statement, 'My father is over eighty and doesn't use glasses. He drinks it straight from the bottle.'

OFFICE ENGLISH Examples galore of this strange vernacular can be encountered on the telephone. Answers to requests to speak to someone take many forms: 'Wud ye wait a wee tick?' 'Did youse ring?' 'Cud ye houl on?' 'He's in but he's gone.' 'Cud ye ring back after a wee while?' 'Will I tell him you called? I will if you like.' 'What are ye? I'll have to say.'

OSTENTATION Considered one of the major sins. The general feeling about it is summed up in the comment heard as a hunt was passing, the huntsmen including a local trader who was considered an upstart: 'Just luck at him. Ridin' along there as if his horse had shit marmalade.'

OVERHEARD Collectors of overheard delights have come to a paradise for the eavesdropper.

Passenger in black taxi: 'When I ast my man if his oul' pipe didden sicken him he said it would sicken him far more if he didden hev it.'

Woman at Belfast airport: 'They asked me if I would like two smokin' seats and I said I didn't mind so long as they didn't go on fire.'

Woman in supermarket: 'Lizzie's in hospital again. She'll not be at herself till she gets her legs back.'

Man in bus queue: 'The wife bought me a digital watch for Christmas. It plays "The Yellow Rose of Texas" at two o'clock in the morning. You never heard the like of it.'

Woman in bus: 'I told Mary her carpet looked lovely down and she said my shoes looked lovely on.'

Shopper in city store: 'I was talking to her next door. She has a knee.'

Customer in post office: 'The wee lad got a postcard from his aunt telling him to write soon. He sent her one back with the word "soon" on it.'

Woman shopper: 'My mother's not well at all. She's going down the drain so she is.'

"SHE'S GOIN' DOWN THE DRAIN, SO SHE IS"

In a public library: 'My man says a good hysterical novel is hard to beat.'

Woman in post office queue: 'Which trap should I go to? I want to know if you need a licence for a shooting stick?'

Customer in chemist's: 'The dacter said it was an infection and he gave be penniskillen for it.'

Lisburn woman to neighbour: 'In the summer if you put the butter out it runs away and if you put it in the fridge it gets as hard as a brick. A body doesn't know where to turn.'

Girl in city office: 'I asked her if she could squeeze another cup out of the teapot and she said, "Why, is it rubber?"'

Bus passenger to companion: 'The man asked me what I meant

when I said I wanted flires and I told him they were what you get in bookies.'

Woman in bus queue: 'The child kept us awake the whole night with abominable pains.'

Newspaper seller's advice to woman about to cross a busy street: 'Watch yerself, missus. You'd get a bumful of tin there very quick.'

Woman describing a visit to a neighbour, a chronic borrower: 'I had one look round me and, do you know, I felt more at home in that house that I do in my own.'

Ballyclare woman to friend: 'I sent the wee lad for a six-inch flower pot and he said he wasn't able to find one. The only ones in the shop had holes in them.'

Man in newsagent's: 'The wee lad kept sayin' he was freezin' an I warmed his ear.'

Woman in village shop: 'She clapsed in the kitchen and she's gettin' buried on Friday. Her other son's a plasterer.'

Laden city shopper: 'That swimsuit my daughter bought herself is only a hair's breadth from the nude. It's this television.'

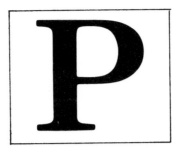

PAN One of the most used kitchen utensils; no housewife could do without one.

'I just fried the pan for our tea', denotes a meal of fried eggs, bacon, sausages and fried bread. 'I'd be up the creek without the pan', points to an exorbitant addiction.

It is an essential element in an 'Ulster fry', in equal demand after a day's work or at the end of a round of golf. The man who declares, 'I'm sick of the pan', is in a critical condition, liable to be in need of intensive care. He faces near starvation. However, the Shankill Road threat, 'I'll knock your pan in', implies the use of physical force, not an intention to cause havoc in a kitchen.

'I married a pan man', denotes (a) despair that the speaker is doomed to live with a person with a one track mind when it comes to food, or (b) the gloom of a vegetarian at the prospect of having to stare at sizzling eggs and bacon for the remainder of her days.

'I'm ready for the pan,' conveys the simple message, 'I'm starving.'

Wives will say, 'My man wouldn't go content to his work or his darts without the pan', and, 'When he comes in from the brew he's the happy man when he smells the pan.'

Families can differ in frying techniques. One will insist that the soda bread is fried and toasted in the fat, another's taste will be to 'give it a wee rummle round the pan', while some will prefer the rule, 'Don't split the farl but fry it well.' In the same category are those who say, 'Don't forget the pirta and do it on both sides.'

PETS In many cases the choice of a family pet can indicate social status. Budgies are a popular working-class choice. Attachment to them can be intense. A woman asked a shopkeeper, 'Could you give me something for our wee budgie. Its hair keeps falling out. Its driving us astray.' Another declared, 'Our budgie can't stand Channel 4. If you're watching it and the cover isn't on the cage it can change to BBC1 without you doing a thing. I wonder why it is?'

"HE'S THE HAPPY MAN WHEN HE SMELLS THE PAN"

(It was established by a television engineer that the cage was close to the set, that there was a loose connection, and that when the bird flapped its wings unduly it was enough to cause the change.)

Canaries and goldfish are prized as pets in many working-class homes. One Belfastwoman told a friend, 'We just had to get rid of our three wee goldfish. My man said he was sick of them snappin' at him every night. It broke my heart so it did.'

Dogs are liked by all classes, with the larger breeds often favoured as status symbols. A woman summed up her feelings about them by saying, 'We gat a wee dog to yep at strangers. He's a great wee animal.'

The high figures at which pigeons can change hands reflect their popularity. They are often prized by those with back-yards rather than back gardens. One pigeon widow lamented, 'Know what I'm going to tell you? I sometimes think I'd be far better aff in a home. All I do is keep feedin' that man of mine so he can get away to feed his oul' pigeons.'

PLACE NAMES There are many traditional rhymes associated with towns, townlands and villages. Many echo old coaching days, but are still remembered and still quoted:

Portavogie is a poor wee hole,
They burn the wrack to save the coal;
They drink salt water to save sweet milk
And they're the boys who can wear the silk.

The measurements seems to have gone wrong somewhere in:

From Augher by Clogher to Fivemiletown
Its six miles up and seven miles down
From Cullyhanna to Crossmaglen
You'll find more rogues than honest men.

There are many variations of one rhyme, depending on the origins of the person quoting it:

Lisnaskea for drinking tea,
Maguiresbridge for brandy,
Tempo is a dirty wee hole
But Rosslea is a dandy.

Another version runs:

Augher, Clogher, Fivemiletown,
Tempo is the cleanest town,
Pettigo for bottled stout
But Bangor's full of hooks and touts.

The rhymers leave few stones unturned in their efforts:

Toome for poteen,
Cookstown for stout,
Ardglass for herrings
And lie-abouts.
Ballycastle for yellow man,
Bangor for girls who want a man,
Ballyclare so sweet and fair,
Bangor for lads with Mohican hair,
Belfast for pubs that are never without,
Ballymena with nothing for nowt.

There are few places without their own special rhymes, some flattering, some denigratory:

Magheramorne for pigs and sows,
Ballygowan for brandy,
Moneyrea for baps and tay
But Cummer is the dandy.

The last line gives the dialect rendering for 'Comber'. In fact it is the Gaelic word for it.

POLAR Form of headgear; often known as a 'hard hat', more generally a bowler. A must for most funerals but now going out of fashion. Obligatory wear in a number of Orange Lodges for Twelfth of July parades. Often white gloves will also be favoured.

A woman will say, 'My man always lucks funny in his wee polar walkin' behine a hearse', but this will not induce him to discard it.

A Belfast firm kept a store of around a dozen polars in various sizes for use by executives when attending the funerals of employees. Otherwise they were never used.

Formerly the badge of office of shipyard foremen, gas meter inspectors and some bank messengers. In industry, 'protective headgear' has taken its place.

POLES A sport with a considerable and dedicated following. A variant of the crown poles played in England. In recent years there has been increasing support for poles under cover.

A Belfastwoman, asked if her husband was at home, explained, 'He's away out for a game of indoor poles.'

A keen polar will usually be 'known to take a drink'. Generally he is more interested in soccer than in rugby, squash or golf, and faithful about filling in pools coupons.

Considered by the retired and senior citizens to have definite advantages over more energetic sporting activities like athletics and motor-cycle racing.

POMEROY Town in Co. Tyrone liable to surprise the motorist in search of petrol. If a garage attendant asks, 'What breed does she run on?' he is trying to establish whether four star, three star or two star petrol is sought.

If the motorist stops at a pub in nearby Sixmilecross to buy a drink he may face the following inquiry when being served: 'Have ye enough thinners?' This means, 'Are you all right for mixers?'

PORN IJIT Not to be confused with pornography, merely descriptive of a person incapable of rational behaviour or thought, as in, 'The fella's a porn ijit. Says the pan for breakfast in the mornin' can damage your health'; 'Joe says the wee Glens is the goat's toe. He's a porn ijit'; 'I knew he was a porn ijit when I heard he tuk his missus to the dogs with him'; 'Alec's a porn glype. Spoke back to his morr-in-law.'

(see IJIT)

POST OFFICE A paradise for connoisseurs of overheard gems: 'I always get my stamps at the counter because they're fresher than the ones from the machine'; 'The wife said the stamp wouldn't stick to the envelope and I told her she'd licked it too much'; 'I asked for a left hand stamp and the man give me a luck. I only wanted to send the letter by air mail.'

POTATOES Prominent on every shopping list. Anyone called Murphy faces the inevitable nickname, 'Spud Murphy' spuds being known as 'murphies'.

The most commonly told potato story concerns the Ulsterman on holiday in England who complained about his boarding house dinner. When invited to explain what was wrong with it he retorted, 'Wrang with it? What was right with it? Only twa tatties, yin of them bad and the ither an onion.'

A lament heard in a cafe was, 'I asked for boiled potatoes and they brought me fried. Wouldn't you call that a raw deal?'

In Fermanagh can be heard the criticism, 'She's as ignorant as priddy bread at a weddin'.'

Potato farls are sometimes served with apple fillings, but these are for epicures, not gluttons. In rural areas the custom of carrying around a slice of raw potato is reckoned to ward off rheumatism. A cure for warts is to rub them with a piece of raw potato, then bury the potato.

Ways of preparing potatoes are many and varied. A tourist, describing a call at a cottage near Strangford, Co. Down, to ask for hot water to make tea, reported: 'The aged tenant asked us, "How would you like a pot of new boiled potatoes?" We jumped at the idea and watched as she filled a three-legged pot and put it on to boil. When the potatoes were almost ready she emptied out the water and covered the potatoes with several sheets of newspaper, then replaced the lit. After about five minutes the pot was removed from the fire and the potatoes turned out on to a large plate, dry and floury and bursting out of their skins. We bought a print of butter from her and we will never forget the delicious flavour of those potatoes as we sat on the sandy beach nearby and devoured them.'

PRAISE This is rarely indicated directly, but can nevertheless be sincerely meant. Examples are: 'If trouble flies in through the windy his hand is the first on the latch'; 'He's never behind the door if your cow's in the sheugh'; 'She'll always give you the len' of her smoothin' iron with a heart and a half'; 'His religion never comes aff with his Sunday suit'; 'He's never a man who would keep the top of the milk to himself.'

PRIDE Shown by many housewives in their concern about the appearance of their living conditions. Typical is the Co. Tyrone woman who got some new kitchen chairs. The children were forbidden to sit on them and had their meals standing at the table in case the chairs might be 'scuffed'.

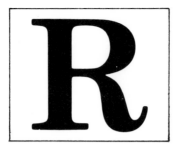

The letter 'R' is constantly ignored in everyday speech. 'On the other side of the Border' becomes, 'On the other side of the Boda.'

Commonly heard are: 'He used theatnin' language'; 'I thew it out'; 'My stummick thinks my thote's cut'; 'He doesn't thill me any more'; 'I feel as if I'm goin to tho aff.'

The usage sometimes figures in advice tendered to a boxer taking a hammering, as in, 'Tho inna tile.'

References to the 'Ministay of Health' will be heard, as well as to the Guvament'.

ROMANCE Dashing Lotharios will not be encountered at every street corner or crossroads. They are more liable to surface in a lounge bar than in an ordinary pub.

Behaviour in affairs of the heart is generally governed by a mixture of caution, prudence and circumspection rather than impetuousness and brinkmanship.

One suitor was spending a week-end at his loved one's home in the country to meet her parents. At bedtime she told him, 'We don't get up early on Sunday so just lie on till you hear me scraping the toast.' She could never understand why he lost interest from that moment.

A country girl out driving with her sweetheart on an icy, wintry evening complained: 'Just look at my hands. They're blue with the cold.' 'Why can't you sit on them, then?' he replied.

A couple out for a walk had come to recognise that their affections were cooling. An attractive girl passed and the man said, 'Did you see that? She smiled at me.' 'That's nothing,' came the reply. 'The first time I saw you I laughed out loud.'

Evidence that not all men are 'cold fish', or dour wooers, is provided by the Armagh man, rejected after years of courtship, who said, 'I headed there and then for the lough. I sat on the bank in the light of the moon, took off my shoes and socks, and washed my

"LET'S GO INTO THE SIN ROOM"

hands and feet clean of her, so I did.'

ROOM Describes a wide variety of domestic accommodation, especially rural. 'A sin room' is not one used for immoral purposes. It is simply the sitting room, often designated 'the lounge'.

In working-class homes 'the room' is also called the 'parlour'.

'The room's done' indicates that the bed has been made in the room reserved for anyone who might stay overnight.

'There's no room in the house' need not denote anything more than that the rooms are fairly small.

In country areas 'the room' is the show room of the house, reserved strictly for clerical visitations or other important occasions, often for writing a letter. It is usually kept locked, with no admission for children.

There could be no higher tribute than, 'You should see the room in her house. You could ate your dinner off the floor.'

SCALLIONS When abroad, Ulster people run into problems when they ask for scallions at a greengrocer's. These, of course, are known elsewhere as spring onions. In fact the Hebrew equivalent of the term is 'onions of Askelon'. 'Scallions' is clearly a corruption of 'Askelon'.

SCHOOL An important element in the background of the average native. If it is established that he is a *'Stonian* it means he has been educated at the Royal Belfast Academical Institution, often referred to as *Inns*. *Stonians* consider themselves superior to those educated at *Mehadie*, or Methodist College, frequently spoken of as *Clejins*, or *Cambill*, which means Campbell College.

It is safe to assume that all play rugby, cricket, squash, monopoly, golf and bridge, abhor 'Top of the Paps' and travelling in buses, and are liable to call their wives 'honeybunch', although 'she' is sometimes used.

SHOPPING An activity which can have unusual motives. A woman will buy a new coat 'just to have it'. A Belfast trader was asked for 'a pair of men's trunks with legs in them.' Cakes will be bought 'in case somebody comes', i.e. so that they can be produced as evidence of the lavish life-style of the householder. A motorist in search of a map was shown several varieties of floor mops.

A village grocer who was asked for 'a pound of hard apples for Sybil' knew immediately what was meant. Sybil was the name of the shopper's goat. The animal would not stand still while being milked unless it had an apple to munch. One hard apple was sufficient for a quart of milk.

A Belfast shopper seeking enough wool to knit a winter coat for her pet dog was told that a better idea of the amount of wool required might be obtained if the dog were brought along. 'But I couldn't do that,' came the protest. 'I want it to be a surprise for the wee pet.'

A country draper was confronted by a customer who wanted 'a blue nightdress with long sleeves, for I throw my arms out of the bed at night and they get cold.'

A shopkeeper was asked, 'Is them eggs fresh?' and replied, 'I ain't saying they ain't.' Retorted the shopper, 'I ain't asking you is they ain't. I'm asking you is they is, is they?'

An Ulsterwoman on holiday in Scotland admired a set of antlers in an antique shop and asked the price. '£25,' she was told. 'They're offa dear,' she commented. 'Of course they're off a deer,' she was told. 'Did you think they were off a greyhound?'

It is part of the shopkeeper's life to be confronted with strange requests, such as, 'I want a pair of scissors that would cut my toes,' and 'Have you a pilla for a dive-in bed?'

Ordering carrots, a shopper said, 'I want the ones in Titchy Beggs.' The baffled shopkeeper explained that he knew of no one of that name who owned a shop. 'But you know what I mean,' persisted the shopper, 'Wee Titchy Beggs.' Finally all was made clear. What was wanted were pre-packed carrots in tissue bags.

SODA BREAD

Soda bread is not now baked at home as often as formerly. Before the home-made variety has entirely vanished, here is the recipe:

Take 2lbs flour, 1 teaspoon bicarbonate of soda, 1 heaped teaspoon salt, 1½ozs butter or margarine, 1 pint buttermilk. Sift together the flour, salt and bicarbonate of soda into a large mixing bowl. Rub in the butter and mix with the buttermilk into a good soft dough. Transfer to a floured board and flatten out to about two inches thick, shape round, then cut into four quarters or farls. These are put onto a hot, ungreased griddle and cooked on a low, steady heat for 12 to 15 minutes on each side.

SPEECH

The diversity and capriciousness of the vernacular fills the air with rich, colourful language. A visitor, admiring a National Trust garden, was told, 'You want to be here in the summer when the beds is black with yellow roses.'

A woman rushed into a village grocery and called out, 'Givvus a tin of calves' milk in a hurry for the bus. I'm takin' the chile till the clink.'

Agreement with a statement will come in the form of, 'It is that', but 'I hear ye' signifies a high degree of doubt over what has been heard.

A mother will complain: 'They giv the childern burney sweets. It didden do their wee gubs any good.'

A comment will run: 'She has awful nice dark hair. Pity she made such a haun of herself.'

A farm visitor heard the loud cackling of a hen and asked, 'Is that hen lyin'?' He was instructed: 'Go on out an luck for yerself. Ye'll soon know if she has laid or lied.'

The statement, 'They are no leavin' there any more', infers that the people in question have moved house.

'Me and her's very big,' signifies close friendship.

'I wed the lawn' or 'I wed the beds' is not an indication that something has been weighed.

A passer-by, criticising the animals illustrated on the ceramic wall tiles at a butcher's, said, 'Them sheeps is awful bad drew.'

'I dropped her a hint but she never lifted it', is synonymous with the lady's inability to get the message.

A child will be warned: 'Don't speak to strangers unless you know them.'

'It's more ornamental than useful, like the curl on a pig's tail,' signifies disapproval.

'I wouldn't put it past him,' adds up to a verdict that the person alluded to is not to be trusted.

A new postman delivering a badly addressed letter was told it should be left at 'the house with the fir trees at the bottom of the road.' Later he complained to his informant: 'I had to give up. I could only see a house with two trees. There was none with four.' 'I know,' came the reply. 'I said the house with the two fir trees.'

An 80-year-old confessed: 'At my time of life you get a lot of them wee bothers that crop up. If you're no drippin' at the snoot you've twitches roun' the sholters an aboot the legs.' His listener, an Englishman, asked what was meant by snoot and was told, 'Ach ye hev yin yersel, man, right in the middle of your face, an' mine you it's a right wheeker.'

An elderly lady on the beach at Scarborough asked an Ulster visitor the time and was told, 'Ten past eight.' 'What's eight?' she wanted to know. The Ulsterman showed her his watch. 'I see what you mean,' said the woman, 'Ten past ite.'

A farmer's wife was about to have a baby and at around two o'clock in the morning her husband hurriedly set off to fetch the midwife. He knocked urgently at her window and when she called, 'Who's there?' he explained his mission. She said, 'All right. I'll be down in a minute.' He replied, 'Well, don't be long for I have my hat in my haun.'

The owner of a seaside guest house was telephoned with a request for a bedroom with a bath and toilet. 'I'm sorry,' he replied, 'I don't have one with a toilet, but I could let you have a room that overlooks the sea.'

A joiner, admiring a tight mortis and tenor joint, said, 'It's as tight as a fish's arse and it's watertight.' Discussing different hardwoods such as teak or ebony, he said, 'It's as hard as a hoor's heart.' Assessing different types of glue with a colleague, he said of a new variety, 'It sticks like shit tae a blanket.'

SPORT The popularity of sports in Ulster is reflected by the fact that, whatever the game, it is capable of exciting comment at its most mordant from those following it. No fans are more explicit. Nor, indeed, more artless. Typifying the quality of some of the criticisms is this conversation between two spectators after their team had been overwhelmed:

'Our left-half left the other half at home.'

'And the centre-half only got one kick at the ball and it was a header.'

'Aye, and missed it. Our goalie would have been better with a corner flag stuck in the middle of the goal.'

'He's getting a transfer to Notts Forest. He should do well sawing down the trees.'

'Going to see the team again next week?'

'Wouldn't miss it. Sure they're not a bad wee side.'

A selection of the sayings of sports fans comes from Malcolm Brodie, much-travelled sports editor of the *Belfast Telegraph*:

At the time the death of Gigli, the Italian tenor, was being announced, Northern Ireland and Italy were playing at Windsor Park. It was a fiercely fought match and feelings were running high, when an Italian player was ordered off for a tackle on an Irish

back. As the offender was leaving the field a Belfast voice roared out, 'Put him in a box along with Gigli.'

Seeking to goad an opponent in a pub argument, a soccer fan exclaimed, 'Anyway, we've no Fenians on our team.' Quietly came the reply, 'Lucky Fenians.'

After a rough Linfield game with a Turkish team a home supporter was heard inquiring 'Them Turks—are they Prod Muslims or Catholic Muslims?'

An Irish supporter at the 1982 World Cup in Spain who was ordering two bottles of 'San Miguel' beer, addressed the waiter, *'Señor*, sir, two "Sammy Magills", *monsieur.'*

When German journalists were being given an outline of the Irish team's tactical plan they were told, 'Our whole idea is to equalise before the other team scores.'

During an Irish Football Association Council discussion one of the speakers, a constant interruptor, was told from the chair, 'Sit down or I'll have to bring my gravel down on you.'

Boxing produces barracking no less caustic than soccer. At an Ulster Hall tournament a spectator, whose view of the ring was being constantly upset by photographers' flash-bulbs, called out indignantly, 'Throw them bloody welders outa here.'

Requests to 'Start the dance music' or 'Put the lights on—I'm reading' during contests marked by lack of excitement are inevitable.

On the day when Prince Charles was being invested as Prince of Wales, Ireland beat Wales by over sixty shots in a bowls international at Mortlake. A youth studying the scoreboard was heard to murmur, 'Not much of a start for Charlie on his first day.'

An Irish supporter at another bowls international in England telephoned from his room in desperation to complain to the hotel receptionist: 'I can't find the zip in my sleeping bag.' It was pointed out that the 'sleeping bag' was, in fact, a duvet.

When snooker star Ray Reardon was told of the banning of Belfastman Alex Higgins for licking the ball before the start of a frame, he was heard to ask, 'Who would touch anything Alex licked?'

Another Ulster snooker star, Denis Taylor, after appearing in specially designed glasses, explained: 'Now I can see the pots I miss.'

A Belfastman, travelling home after a Dundalk race meeting at which he lost practically all his money, was passing the city cemetery, where one of his closest friends had been buried only a few days before. He was unable to resist calling out, 'Don't worry, Hughie. You're missin' nathin' here.'

STAR CRAVEN MAD A phrase often applied to soccer referees considered to be ineffectual. It implies that he is stark raving mad and should be returned to the mental institution from which he had been let out.

A person can be *star craven mad* who expects a dry and sunny 'Twelfth', or announces he has agreed to his wife attending further education classes in Urdu, decides to buy 'a wee dug for company', or announces that he intends to 'take up palitics to pass the time.'

STARING A well-established custom, commonly described as *stern*. If you are a confirmed starer and are sitting in a crowded bus, your day is made. Your victims have no escape. Your subjects can include people wearing odd socks, someone pregnant, with a squint or ill-fitting teeth, a woman in a mink jacket, a woman wearing curlers, or anyone overdressed.

The starer can silently but effectively indicate distaste, resentment, contempt, amusement, or pity. The greater the discomfort shown by the victim, the greater the enjoyment of the starer.

If you are 'a staree' you go through agonies of remorse that you didn't wear a better suit, polish your shoes, get your hair done, spend more time with your make-up or change your socks.

Starers are responsible for governing many aspects of behaviour and dress. It is common to reason, 'If I wear an outfit like that people will stare.'

There are grounds for the argument that staring should be made an offence against the law. The challenge, 'Who do you think you're staring at?' has started many a fight. This can happen when one starer is confronted by another.

Staring is a practice at which children are particularly skilled One small boy, warned that picking his nose would give him an enormous stomach, was fascin- ated by a woman in an advanced state of pregnancy sitting near him in a bus. Finally he exclaimed, 'Hi, missus, I know what you've been at.'

A woman hobbled into a Donaghadee surgery with her knee bandaged, a black eye, and several cuts and bruises. When asked, 'What would seem to be the trouble?' she replied, 'People keep staring at me, doctor.'

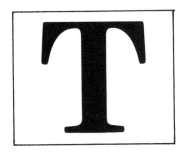

TEA Part and parcel of Ulster life. With some reason it could be said, 'The place is coming down with vivid tea drinkers.' Lack of awareness of this can confuse visitors, hence the case of the Englishwoman who was asked, 'Would you like a mouthful in your hand?' and replied, 'I wouldn't mind only I have my gloves on.' The hostess looked at her as if she had taken leave of her senses.

In many cases, 'a good cup of tea' is assessed as one on which 'a 10p piece would float.'

Tea buffs have been known to make such requests as, 'Cud ye squeeze anor cup outa the teapot?' and to make statements like, 'I threw the teapot out and forgot it had a coupla cups in it.'

It is not considered unusual for a mother to call to her child playing in the street, 'Come in fer yer tea. Spored.'

'The tea's drew', infers that a meal is ready, 'a drappa scald' is synonymous with 'a cup for drinking'.

Two extremes in tea-making are covered by the statements, 'I like tea you could trot a mouse across' and, 'It was that wake you could read the paper through it.'

Voicing appreciation of a well-brewed cup, a woman said, 'I needed that to rinse the wine away.' (It acted as a remedy for her flatulence.)

A woman complained to a neighbour, 'There I was, just settlin' down for a crack and a cuppa tea in wee Mrs Cairns's when I happened to remark as she was pouring it out, "It looks like rain." Talk about the look she gave me, but mind you the second cup was an awful lot stronger.'

A visitor was told apologetically, 'I was just going to make you a wee cup but the teapot run out on me.'

The statement, 'the tea's not right drew', affirms that it needs a few minutes before being poured.

TEETH Frequent topic of comment, especially when dentures are worn. A woman said, 'My man has more teeth in his head than the mouth of a flour bag.' This was a mere statement of fact, a

68

recognition that here was something he had to learn to live without.

A wedding guest said after the reception: 'I did so not enjoy it, for I never minded my teeth till we set down.'

When a house guest was asked if she had slept well in spite of the crying of another guest's baby in the next room, she relied, 'Sure when I take my teeth out I can't hear a thing.'

Despair was voiced by a Tyrone woman who insisted, 'My man's an awful nuisance in bed at night.

He's for ever wantin' me to reach him his teeth to bite my ears, the oul' ijit.'

THREATS Stern warnings to ill-behaved children formerly took a much more bloodthirsty form than those of today, which usually run to, 'I'll send you to your bed if you don't stop being a nuisance.'

Threats that can still be remembered by older generations were often a variant of, 'If you come home with a broken leg I'll wring your wee neck.' These were rarely taken seriously, nor was it intended that they should.

Hardly in this category, however, were warnings like, 'If you don't do what you're told I'll whitewash the kitchen with your blood'; 'Take anything more that doesn't belong to you and it won't be the police I'll send for, it'll be an ambulance'; 'I'll give you such an uppercut that you won't come down for a week if you don't stop aggravating me'; 'If you go on acting the lig I'll bate you round the balls of the leg with a teaspoon.'

One Co. Antrim admonition was: 'You keep away from that well. You could be drowned in it and anyway it's full of wee popes.'

A Belfast mother's reprimand was: 'If you don't stop botherin' me I'll pull your ears off and fry them in the pan for your dinner.'

TOILET Never in any circumstances referred to as the 'comfort station', but will sometimes be designated as 'the bog'.

There are instances where 'the toilet' is understood without actually being named. A man shopping with his little daughter in a city store felt her tugging at his sleeve and heard her whisper urgently, 'I have to go, daddy.' A woman assistant standing nearby sized up the situation and said to the man's relief, 'I'll take her along.' When they returned father beamed his appreciation and said to the little girl, 'I hope you thanked the lady.' Eagerly the youngster answered, 'Why, daddy, she had to go too.'

TRAFFIC Crossing signals have brought their own problems to those pedestrians who tend to be bewildered by heavy traffic.

A Ballyclare woman illustrated this confusion by rushing up to a group waiting for the lights to change at a busy Bangor crossing. 'Are you people waiting for a funeral?' she wanted to know. 'We're waiting for the red man,' she was told. 'What, a red Indian?' she gasped. 'We're waiting for him to turn green,' came the information. 'I never heard the like,' she objected. 'I'm going to go across anyway.' 'If you do that you'll go to a funeral all right,' she was warned, 'only you won't smell the flowers.' 'Where will I be going, then?' she asked. 'That depends on how you have lived.' 'Well, where is this red man?' she demanded. 'I cannae see one.' At that moment the crowd moved

70

forward. 'Sure I see what you mean,' she exclaimed. 'Why didn't you tell me the first time?'

Similar confusion led a Belfast woman to comment about a friend: 'She stood waiting to cross for hours for she's colour blind and between green men and red ones and them yella lines it's a miracle she ever gets anywhere, the sowl.'

TURN Can describe changing one's religion, a music hall item, or going round a corner.

'He turned' means that the person concerned has decided to subscribe to a different faith, and implies that he is not to be trusted.

A girl receiving a proposal of marriage who asks the proposer, 'Wud ye turn?', is trying to establish if he will adopt her religious beliefs and abandon his own.

The lover who agrees 'to turn' proves his sincerity as effectively as if he signs a declaration in blood.

'A quare turn' indicates a person who can be the life and soul of a party, while 'a bit of a turn' can also signify a sudden bout of illness.

TYRONE, COUNTY (population 139,037). The people are usually hospitable but tend to be rather suspicious of city folk. Their open-handed nature is echoed by the words:

Sit up to the hate, me darlin' Kate
An make yerself at home.

It reflects the same degree of warmth as the welcome, 'Come in, Dungannon, I know your knock.' The speech here is generally rich and lively.

Tyrone claims the old man who said, 'It was that coul', a hadda strip the back o' the dure.' (That is, he had to remove the coats hanging on the door and put them on the bed to warm him at night.)

ULSTERMAN The working-class Ulsterman has a wry sense of humour, often razor sharp. He can show truculence if he feels the occasion demands it but is basically reticent, and tends to convey diffidence about his image.

He will admit he 'doesn't know his Bible' as well as his father did, and has an ability to say of someone, 'He's a bitter wee Prod' in a tone of despair. He has an enthusiasm for bowling and/or Gaelic, depending on the district in which he lives.

He can throw a useful dart and is a different person after two or three pints. He often has a close friend called Jimmy, Alec or Malky whom he will constantly quote, particularly if they are fans of the same soccer/Gaelic player.

If he lived in England he would vote Labour yet consider Arthur Scargill 'a head case'.

If he labels someone 'a dirty yella rat', he will show a readiness to 'kick the fella's slats in'.

Depending on the school he went to, he will think with longing of the days when 'the Yard' was a hive of industry, or voice delight that those days have gone.

He will tell you, 'I went to the hairdresser's and got a clatter weak daff' and watch to see if you smile. (He is describing a severe hair cut.)

Whatever his form of worship, he is devoted to 'the pan', and will sing 'The Sash', 'Kevin Barry' or 'Danny Boy' with the least encouragement, his choice governed by where he worships.

If his wife is pregnant he will say, 'She's thon way' not, 'She's up the spout'. He will refer to her as 'the wife' or 'the missus', rarely 'my wife'.

Only infrequently would it occur to him to buy her flowers and he usually considers it improper to push the pram or the buggy when out for a walk.

He is not unduly bothered if his wife appears at breakfast loaded down with curlers, but feels uncomfortable if she has a good job.

She, too, has a lively sense of humour and would appreciate the story of the neighbour who was admiring a friend's eighteen-month-old baby. The question was asked, 'What do you call him?' The mother answered, 'Nathan', which brought the surprised comment: 'But, my Gawd, at that age surely ye must give the wee lad a name.'

She is often a frenzied knitter and will boast quietly of the things she can 'knit out of my head'.

She will display a neat sense of detail when telling a story. For example: 'A woman I know bought a chinky and when she got it home she found a clack in it; when she looked there wasn't a leg missin'.' This affirms a close knowledge of natural history, and admiration that the lady concerned should be aware of the exact number of legs possessed by a cockroach.

UPBRINGING Family discipline varies extensively, ranging from the severe to the benign. A lot will depend on how the parents themselves were brought up. Typical of the authoritarian is the mother who was told that her small boy had fallen in the street and was 'roaring his head off'. Her reply was, 'Let him cry away there. The more he cries the less he'll pee.'

In the same bracket was the mother who had taken her young son to school for the first time. On arrival he refused to go any further and started weeping. Angrily she told him, 'Am I to leave you with a kiss or a sore behine.'

This contrasts with the father who said of his son's misbehaviour, 'Let the wee lad be. Sure I was young myself once.'

Youngsters who have been 'well brought up' are generally disliked by their peers, and are often labelled 'cissies'.

WAKE Occasion for a night-long assessment of the deceased's life, for gloom as well as joy, but now less religiously observed by city folk than in rural districts. Usually marked in the latter by a generous supply of drink. Custom insists it is unlucky to turn anyone away from a wake, whether or not they are 'friends of the corpse'. This results in considerable abuse of hospitality. The attendance can thus include, 'the corpse's cistern-law, the corpse's bror-in-law, the corpse's cousin, two of the corpse's far-out cousins, frens of the corpse but no relations, and fellas there for the drink.'

When a widow was asked for one of her late husband's shirts to make a shroud she said, 'Divil the white shirt had he', and produced a white underslip, well starched, with lace trimming on the neck and hem. 'Try that on him,' she said. 'It will do him fine well. It's myself that knows it. Every time I wore it a bline man could see the love light in his een.'

Another widow who was asked why she delayed calling the doctor explained, 'Roun' here we cure the sick werselves.' When questioned how this was done she said, 'We make the best poteen and give the sick a glass. If that doesn't work we give him another. If he still isn't better we give him another. If even that's no manner of use, well, they're not worth curin'.'

Of a man survived by four sons it was aid, 'Sure there isn't wan of them boys with the head to fill his shoes.'

Said a mourner of her deceased neighbour, 'He's the nicest corpse I've ever set eyes on. He was over six fut tall an a quare nice wee man.'

A new arrival at a wake was told by the relict, 'I asked the doctor what did he die of and he said it was mainly senility. I told him if the sowl hadn't been so stubborn he wouldn't have had it if he'd let me get the doctor sooner. He wasn't able to get it intil his saucepan head that a man has to go sometime.'

Of a confirmed agnostic who had 'passed on', a mourner said, 'He's brave and well-dressed to be goin' nowhere.'

Another widow expressed her feelings thus: 'Sure it wouldn't have been so bad if he'd waited till the weather turned a bit warmer. He won't feel the cold where he's going, but I'll have to go to the expense of buying myself an electric blanket.'

One mourner concluded his appraisal by saying, 'It was awful sudden, right enough. Many a good handshake he had in his time because of his decency. Now he's finished up with the last yin, a clap on the face with a spade.'

A surprise inquiry by one mourner was, 'Are they hevvin' a post mortal?'

The qualities of one departed friend inspired the tribute, 'There was no harm in the man at all. He had a heart of corn and that's no chaff.'

Still observed at many wakes is the custom of touching the corpse. This is said to prevent you from dreaming of the deceased.

WEATHER A perpetual subject of discussion. It can be, 'a gran day for the ducks', 'a watry mornin', a day calling for the comment 'scummin' down', or 'a snifter of a night'.

The statement, 'the wire's tarble' signifies weather at its worst, while 'cat wire' is another way of saying that it is catastrophic. *Mizzlin* and *drizzlin* are less desirable conditions than *clearn* or *fairn*.

On a bitterly cold day, marked with frequent showers of hail, a housewife hurried to the door to offer shelter to the breadman. The house overlooked a rugby field where a match was in progress. The breadman commented, 'Begod if those boys were working they'd be stannin' shelterin'.'

On a torrid July day a passer-by remarked to a workman slogging away on a Co. Antrim road scheme: 'Hat, issent it?' 'Aye,' he replied. 'The clegs is the buggers a day like that, missus.'

A neighbourly inquiry on a wintry morning, 'How's your man? What about his chest?' brought the reply, 'Augh, this weather'll be the death of him. Ye should hear him haughal in the morning. You'd think it was claps of thunder.'

A Ballyclare man confided to a friend: 'It was that wet a night d'ye know the wife came home w' her backside ringin'.'

WEE SHAP A popular institution, particularly when situated on a corner. There are streets where the *wee shap* has defied the onslaught of the supermarket, largely by keeping open when the supermarket is shut. A wee shap sells nearly everything, from laces to 'brown blacknin', from 'Ferry Lickwood' to candy apples.

There are, of course, limitations, as in the case of the woman who had bought some cocktail sausages and asked the shopkeeper if he had any sticks. 'Sarry, missus,' he replied, 'we've nathin' but firelighters.'

A wee *shap* is unflustered by such requests as, 'Wud ye change that 10p into brown money'; 'Have ye a map head as the hairs are cummin' outa my oul one?' or, 'Hev ye any of that new green smellin' perfume?'

Wee shaps are a sounding board for all kinds of revelations: 'I hate them tea begs. They're useless if ye want to read your cup'; 'I don't know what to make for the dinner. I've turned agin' the pan. Mebbe I'll make a drappa tay in my haun. It might taste my mouth.'

Nine times out of ten *wee shap* proprietors tended to specialise in sweets. These provided all sorts, in every sense.

A woman's recollections of one ran: 'There was no smart window dressing. Indeed the window was always stacked with colourful empty tins. In the *shap* were such delights as 'chew chew', toffee of a delicate rose pink and exquisite flavour, egg and milk 'chew chew', nutty 'chew chew'. The egg and milk flavour was the most popular. With what anticipation we would watch the shopkeeper use his little toffee hammer to measure out our order. Chewing the egg and milk, your mouth would be filled with a creamy, delicious emulsion, sheer bliss to swallow. Swinging on a lamp-post with a mouth full of egg and milk 'chew chew' was heaven itself, and Wagga Wagg's *shap* the gate thereof.'

Memories of a wee Fermanagh *shap* were: 'It could have been there since the first Plantationists made it their rallying point for their few needs. I see yet the yellow tallow candles, ancient wooden bowls, large earthen mugs, stone storage jars, and Mary, the shopkeeper, telling me after fulfilling my order to, 'Watch the step now, daughter', as I would weave my way past bags of corn, bundles of ropes, and salty hard sides of bacon.'

Another recollection was of Candy Mary's, in Belfast's Old Lodge Road. She specialised in home-made slab toffee in six or seven varieties, including peppermint and coconut. Scales were rarely used. Once she was told, 'Please don't give me too much as I'm going back to school.'

In *wee shaps* jam would be sold loose, spooned from an enormous stone jar, also black and white linen thread which hung in hanks and sold in pennyworths.

Mouth-watering merchandise in today's *wee shaps* is different but no less varied. Their candy apples can be highly recommended, as can their toffee, yellow man and other confections—all fighting a losing battle against 'Mars Bars', 'Opal Fruits' and their attractively packaged ilk.

Above all, the *wee shap* is unbeatable when it comes to picking up gossip.

WINDOW SILL Often referred to as 'windy stool', but no longer what it was. Formerly used for the popular children's game of 'dropsies', played with cigarette cards. The object was to touch as many cards as possible with the one you dropped. You collected all those touched.

Often provided a seat for neighbours out for a gossip.

A Twelfth of July tradition is to paint the window sill red, white and blue.

'A day for the windy stool' is one that is warm and sunny.

'A fella fell aff a windy stool' is as commonly used an example of dialect speech as 'a fella fellaff a larry'.

WEDDINGS One unwritten rule about an Ulster wedding is that guests do not go to the nuptials 'on their feet'. Those who walk to the church are considered to lower the tone of the proceedings.

At a Belfast wedding one of the guests made the comment,

'Doesn't the bride look gorgeous?' which brought the reply, 'If you don't look like the Rose of Tralee on your wedding day you have slept in for you won't be worth looking at when you're sitting on the toilet years later with your jaws surrounded with flannel.'

A wedding guest, asked by an usher, 'Who's side are you on?' is not being invited to indicate where his sympathies lie, merely whether he is sitting on the bride's or the bridegroom's side of the church.

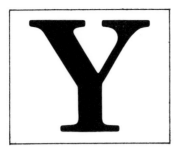

YARD This is Harland and Wolff's famous shipyard, not to be confused with an outside toilet. In its heyday it was a rich source of humour, its output of stories as colourful as its output of great ships.

It was no less rich in characters—men like 'Alec No More', so called because on the day after his promotion to foreman and the accolade of 'a hard hat', a colleague greeted him, 'Hello there, Alec.' 'Luck here,' he replied. 'It's mister from now on. I'm Alec no more.'

A newly-appointed painter was asked on his arrival at work if he had brought his cards. 'I haven't,' he answered, 'but if you like I'll bring a set of draughtsmen and a boord in the morning.'

After nearly forty years service a worker was called aside by his foreman and told, 'I'm very sorry, Bill, you and I will have to part.' 'But where are you going?' he asked 'It isn't me,' the foreman explained, 'it's you, Bill.' It then dawned on him what was happening. 'If I only had known it was a spell job,' he said, 'I'd nivver have

taken it.'

A new foreman, named John Duken, had checked up on his squad, and soon after bumped into a workman a short distance away. 'I'm Duken, the new foreman,' he told the man. 'Just you stick along with me, mate,' the worker said, 'I'm juking him too.'

A shipyardman came upon a friend who was prodding at a deep pool of oily water with a long stick. 'It's my jacket,' he explained. 'It fell in.' 'Man dear, sure it wudden' be worth wearin' if ye ivver got it out,' his friend said. 'Ach, I know,' came the answer, 'but my piece is in the pocket.'

One of the characters still remembered is Big John, a riveter with a prodigious appetite. It was said of him: 'That fella has a stummick like the howl of a boat.'

There are many stories surrounding the ill-fated Belfast-built *Titanic*. Some time after the disaster a riveter is said to have been heard lamenting, 'I knew something would happen to her. A week after she sailed I found twelve rivets in my dungarees I

THE ACCOLADE OF A HARD HAT

clean forgot to put intil her.'

A new employee, told to find the measurements of a steel plate and not accustomed to the use of a rule, came back with the news, 'It's the size of your rule and two thumbs over, with this piece of brick and this bit of a tile, the breadth of my haun and my arm from here to there barn a finger.'

A worker, on being lifted clear after the collapse of a staging, moaned, 'I'm hurt bad. It lucks as if my futball days is over.' 'Ach away, man,' he was told. 'Sure you can still blow a whistle.'

A poor timekeeper was advised to buy a good alarm clock. 'I've got one,' he insisted, 'but it goes aff half an hour before I get up.'

A catchword that lasted for many years was inspired by a foreman who caught a worker boiling his tea-can before the lunch-time horn. The man bolted, leaving the can steaming away. Indignantly, the foreman roared after him: 'I'll boil yer can for ye.'